CW01368998

Rails Through Bala

The Ruabon–Barmouth and Bala–Blaenau Ffestiniog lines
– a photographic history

A. Bodlander, M. Hambly,
H. Leadbetter & D. Southern

*Rails Through Bala, the Ruabon–Barmouth and Bala–Blaenau Ffestiniog Lines
– a photographic history*
First published in Wales in 2011
by
BRIDGE BOOKS
61 Park Avenue
Wrexham
LL12 7AW

© 2011 Photographs, maps and text, A. Bodlander, M. Hambly,
H. Leadbetter and D. Southern
© 2011 Design, typsetting and layout, Bridge Books

All Rights Reserved
No part of this publication may be reproduced,
stored in a retrieval system, or transmitted
in any form or by any means, electronic,
mechanical, photocopying, recording or
otherwise, without the prior permission
of the Copyright holder.

ISBN 978-1-84494-076-9

A CIP entry for this book is available from the British Library

Printed and bound by
Gutenberg Press Ltd
Malta

Contents

Introduction   4
Acknowledgements   6
Map of the railway from Ruabon–Barmouth and   7
Bala–Blaenau Ffestiniog
Chronology   8

Historical background: Ruabon–Barmouth   10
Route description: Ruabon–Barmouth   12
Illustrated history: Ruabon–Barmouth   17

Historical background: Bala–Blaenau Ffestiniog   91
Route description: Bala–Blaenau Ffestiniog   94
Illustrated history: Bala–Blaenau Ffestiniog   96

Bibliography   166

Introduction

Of all Britain's railway companies, the Great Western is generally recognised as the one which put the greatest effort into marketing; promoting the attractiveness of parts of the country served by their network and encouraging tourism through the use of their train and road motor services by sightseers, walkers, golfers and fishermen. In 1906, the Great Western's marketing men coined the term 'The British Tyrol' to describe that part of north Wales served by the company and produced a guide book with that title to whet the appetites of the growing number of town and city dwellers with the time and money to be able to take an annual holiday. The guide book's sub-title 'Through the Marches and the Dee Valley to the Sea' succinctly describes the 54$\frac{1}{2}$-mile route from Ruabon to Barmouth. The preface to the guide book's third edition, published in 1924 during Sir Felix Pole's term as General Manager, concluded thus:

> Year after year, a period of rest and change becomes more and more a necessity of human existence, and the need of holiday-haunts and health- and pleasure-resorts easily accessible and inexpensive grows consequently more urgent and more universal to the busy toilers in great cities. The absorption of the Cambrian Railways by the Great Western Railway under the Railways Act, 1921, has led to an improvement in the already excellent train services to the coast towns of North Wales, while the Festiniog and the Welsh Highlands [sic] narrow-gauge railways, start from near the Portmadoc (GWR) station, and open up the glorious valleys and mountains of Snowdonia. From the experience gained since the close of the Great War it is safe to prophesy that in the near future the Dee Valley and the Country of the Marches – the British Tyrol, in fact – will become one of the most popular of our great national pleasure- and health-giving districts.

The reference to the absorption of the Cambrian is a reminder that the tidy presentation in timetables of services from Ruabon to Barmouth, with connections and through services from London and Birmingham and onwards to Pwllheli, disguises more complex origins. What ultimately became a through route of a little over 50 miles was originally promoted and constructed in five stages and, despite the four locally-promoted companies aligning themselves with the Great Western from the beginning, the Cambrian's ownership of the final stretch to the sea meant that Dolgellau remained a railway 'frontier town' for more than half of the line's lifetime.

Mid-way between Ruabon and Barmouth lies the historic town of Bala, served by a short branch from the through route which was subsequently extended north west, through the mountains to Trawsfynydd and Blaenau

Ffestiniog. These 25 miles were constructed in two stages, with the final few miles from Ffestiniog to Blaenau Ffestiniog being achieved by the conversion of an existing narrow-gauge railway.

In a little over 100 years, the route followed a life cycle seen so often across Britain – promotion, construction, takeover, nationalisation, decline and closure. However, since closure it has also been a double beneficiary of the enthusiasm for railway preservation, with the Llangollen and Bala Lake railways each giving many thousands of holidaymakers the opportunity to sample something of the journey taken by their ancestors through 'The British Tyrol' to fish in the Dee, climb Cader Idris, play golf at Fairbourne or relax on the beach at Barmouth.

It is perhaps fitting that this book was being finalised 50 years after the closure of the Bala to Blaenau Ffestiniog branch at the end of January 1961, four years before services over the through route also ceased. The authors hope that the selection of photographs on the following pages capture something of the atmosphere of both lines for those too young to have seen them in operation, and provide a pleasant reminder of times past for those who were fortunate to have experienced them in operation.

Adrian Bodlander
Mark Hambly
Harry Leadbetter
Dave Southern

January 2011

Note on the use of the Welsh language
The nineteenth-century parliamentary approval process for railway projects which, even though often locally promoted, were frequently closely aligned with English-based railway companies, led to numerous instances of the Welsh language being corrupted in Acts of Parliament, timetables and on station nameboards. Given the historical focus of this book we have used the original titles of railway companies and the spellings of particular station names applicable to the period being described, but when referring to places more generally we have used the spellings in current use e.g. Dolgelly/Dolgelley/Dolgellau and Festiniog/Ffestiniog.

Acknowledgements

The authors are very conscious that the publication of *Rails Through Bala* has only been possible because of the generous support of a number of individuals.

First and foremost are all the photographers who visited the Ruabon–Barmouth and Bala–Blaenau Ffestiniog lines and without whose efforts, and their granting of permission to publish, there would be no book. Wherever possible they have been credited individually but, in a small number of cases, the name of the original photographer has been lost over time, in which case the individual or organisation holding the copy of the photographic print or commercial postcard which has been made available to the authors has been credited.

With the passing of time, the number of surviving railway staff who worked on the lines is dwindling, but we have been very fortunate to be able to speak with Mr John Roberts of Bala who began his railway career at Blaenau Ffestiniog Central and subsequently became a signalman working at a number of the locations featured in this book.

The bibliography recognises the earlier *Rails to Bala* on which two of the present authors collaborated; the previous assistance of their co-authors on that project is acknowledged.

Other snippets of information have come from fellow enthusiasts, too numerous to mention individually, who either travelled on the lines while they were still open, visited after closure or have been involved during the preservation era at Llangollen or Llanuwchllyn.

Our publisher, Alister Williams of Bridge Books, has continued to have confidence in us as a team and has helped fill in the historical and geographical context behind a number of the illustrations.

Last but not least, thanks are due to the wives and daughters who have patiently tolerated the clutter of 'work in progress' and postponement of other tasks during the preparation of this book.

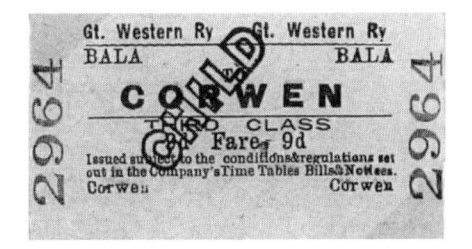

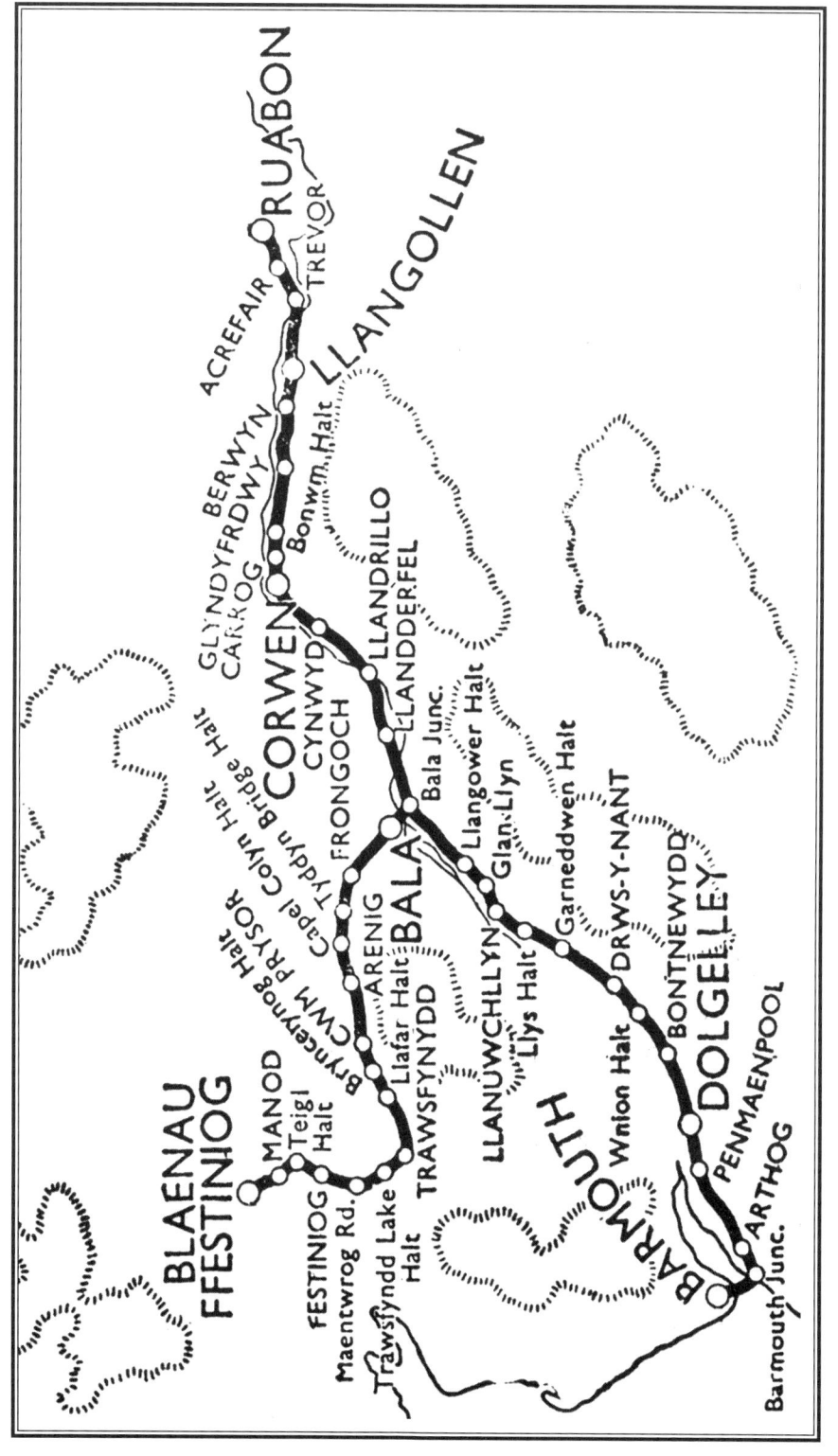

Map of the railway from Ruabon–Barmouth and Bala–Blaenau Ffestiniog

Chronology

1805	Pontcysyllte tramway opened to feed traffic from industries in the Acrefair area to the Llangollen Canal.
1838	Festiniog Railway opened from Blaenau Ffestiniog–Porthmadog.
1846	Chester–Ruabon section of Shrewsbury & Chester Railway opened.
1847	First proposals for a railway to Llangollen as a branch from the Shrewsbury & Chester Railway.
1848	Ruabon–Shrewsbury section of Shrewsbury & Chester Railway opened.
1853	Proposed Denbighshire Railway from Ruabon–Rhyl (via Llangollen and Corwen) promoted.
1859	Construction of Vale of Llangollen Railway between Ruabon and Llangollen begun.
1860	Meetings in Corwen and Bala to discuss proposals for railway links to the Cardigan Bay coast.
1861	Vale of Llangollen Railway opened to goods traffic.
1862	Vale of Llangollen Railway opened to passenger traffic.
1864	Denbigh, Ruthin & Corwen Railway opened to Corwen.
1865	Llangollen & Corwen Railway opened.
1865	Aberystwyth & Welsh Coast Railway branch from Barmouth Junction (Morfa Mawddach)–Dolgellau opened to Penmaenpool.
1865	Proposal for a Bala, Festiniog and Penrhyndeudraeth Railway.
1867	Aberystwyth & Welsh Coast Railway opened between Barmouth Junction and Barmouth, over the Barmouth viaduct.
1866	Corwen & Bala Railway opened between Corwen and Llandrillo.
1868	Remainder of Corwen & Bala Railway opened.
1868	Festiniog and Blaenau Railway opened as a narrow-gauge railway.
1869	Aberystwyth & Welsh Coast Railway opened between Penmaenpool and Dolgellau, marking completion of through route from Ruabon–Barmouth.
1870	Arthog station opened.
1880	Bala Junction station opened.
1882	Bala & Festiniog Railway opened from Bala–Llan Ffestiniog.
1883	Conversion of Festiniog & Blaenau Railway to standard-gauge completed.
1900	Line between Ruabon (Llangollen Line Junction) and Llangollen (Llangollen Goods Junction) doubled.
1908	Passing loop installed at Deeside, between Berwyn and Glyndyfrdwy.
1922	Great Western Railway and Cambrian Railways merge, giving the Great Western ownership of the entire Ruabon–Barmouth route.

1927	Great Western Railway upgrade structures and track between Ruabon and Barmouth from 'Uncoloured' to 'Blue' route classification.
1930s	A number of halts opened on Ruabon–Barmouth and Bala–Blaenau Ffestiniog lines in an attempt to attract additional passengers at a time of increased bus competition.
1948	British railways nationalised.
1960	Bala to Blaenau Ffestiniog closed to passengers.
1961	Bala to Blaenau Ffestiniog closed to goods.
1964	Link between Great Western and London & North Western Railway stations in Blaenau Ffestiniog opened. Line reopened between Blaenau Ffestiniog and Trawsfynydd Power Station siding.
1964	Final through trains run between Ruabon and Barmouth as line is severed by flooding five weeks prior to formal closure.
1965	Withdrawal of passenger service between Ruabon and Barmouth.
1968	Withdrawal of freight services between Ruabon and Llangollen.
1969	Track lifting completed between Llangollen Line Junction (Ruabon) and Morfa Mawddach (Barmouth Junction).
1970	Merioneth County Council consider plans for a narrow-gauge railway from Bala–Morfa Mawddach to run on the former standard-gauge trackbed.
1972	Bala Lake Railway commences operations from Llanuwchllyn.
1975	Llangollen Railway established at Llangollen.
1981	Llangollen Railway operates first passenger trains.
1982	New joint British Rail and Ffestiniog Railway station opened in Blaenau Ffestiniog on site of former Great Western station.
1998	Line between Blaenau Ffestiniog and Trawsfynydd Power Station mothballed following completion of removal of fuel elements after electricity generation ends.
2011	Plans announced for UK's first Velorail operation on mothballed Blaenau Ffestiniog to Trawsfynydd Power Station line.

Historical background: Ruabon–Barmouth

As noted in the introduction, the through route from Ruabon, south of Wrexham on the Great Western's Shrewsbury–Chester line, to Barmouth, on the Cambrian's Coast line (which skirts Cardigan Bay from Dovey Junction to Pwllheli) was originally promoted and constructed in five stages during the 1860s.

The enthusiasm for promoting and building new railways across Britain, the 'Railway Mania', reached a peak in the mid 1840s. The position in north Wales at that time was no exception, with the principal focus of the projects proposed being to accelerate journeys between London and Dublin, either via Holyhead or, in one proposal, via a new port at Porth Dinllaen near Nefyn, on the north coast of the Llŷn peninsula. Proposed routes variously involved extensive tunnelling through the Berwyn Mountains or following Telford's Holyhead road (today's A5) to Capel Curig and then continuing to Bangor via Llanberis or Bethesda.

Not unsurprisingly, none of these schemes came to fruition and it was into the 1850s before more credible proposals were put forward, although these envisaged an 'L-shaped' link between the Shrewsbury–Chester line and the north Wales coast (with Corwen at the corner), rather than striking out towards the Cardigan Bay coast. Ultimately, it was the summer of 1859 before the Vale of Llangollen Railway received parliamentary approval and construction began.

Next came the Llangollen and Corwen Railway, authorised a year after the Vale of Llangollen. The engineering challenges presented by the need to bridge the Dee and tunnel through the northern extremity of the Berwyn Mountains in the first three miles from Llangollen meant that the line to Corwen was not ready for use until mid 1865. The Denbigh, Ruthin and Corwen Railway, which subsequently became part of the London & North Western Railway, had reached the town from the north the previous year.

The Bill authorising the Corwen & Bala Railway received Royal Assent in June 1862. The terrain on this stretch presented fewer challenges, and the section from Corwen–Llandrillo was ready for use in July 1866. The line from Llandrillo onwards, to Bala's first station, was opened in April 1868. The longest of the five components, the Bala & Dolgelly Railway, also received Royal Assent in June 1862 and was opened in August 1868.

Following the authorisation of the Bala & Dolgelly, the Aberystwyth & Welsh Coast Railway, one of the constituents of the Cambrian Railways, was authorised to build a link from their route along the Cardigan Bay coast to follow the southern bank of the Mawddach estuary towards Dolgellau. This reached Penmaenpool in July 1865, but the project then stalled and it was not until June 1869 that the through route was completed.

So, by midsummer 1869, there was a through route from industrial north-east Wales to the Cardigan Bay coast, serving four significant towns en route, each of which gave its name to one or more of the component companies, a situation which prevailed for the next 95^1/$_2$ years. Ownership was tidied up with the Great Western Railway absorbing the Bala & Dolgelly in 1877, and the three companies which built the components along the Dee Valley in 1896. However, it was not until 1922, when the entire route and the lines with which it connected at each end, came under a single umbrella upon the amalgamation of the Cambrian and five south Wales railways with the Great Western, to form an enlarged company. A final change of ownership came about on 1 January 1948 upon nationalisation and the creation of British Railways.

As the pattern of local and through services developed in the second half of the Victorian era, improvements were made to station facilities and signalling, culminating in the doubling of the section from Llangollen Line Junction–Llangollen Goods Junction and the extension of the platforms at Llangollen to accommodate excursion traffic, both of which were ready for use from late 1900.

Additional passing loops at Deeside and Garneddwen were completed before the First World War and then, in the inter-war period, a number of small halts, aimed at attracting both local residents and tourists who might otherwise have made the omnibus their preferred mode of transport, were opened.

The *Reshaping of British Railways* report decreed that there only needed to be one through route to the Cardigan Bay coast and the route from Shrewsbury was ultimately selected. Closure was eventually set for Monday, 18 January 1965, the same as for the Cambrian main line between Whitchurch and Buttington Junction (Welshpool) and the Llanfyllin Branch.

Route description: Ruabon–Barmouth

The journey to Barmouth typically began from the bay platform on the west side of Ruabon station, although over the years a number of through services originated further north at Wrexham General, Chester General or Birkenhead Woodside and so would have instead run through the up main platform.

For a little over half-a-mile trains ran south on the Shrewsbury & Chester Railway main line before branching off to the west at Llangollen Line Junction, a conventional double-line junction. All distances on the line were measured in miles and chains from this junction.

The line then climbed at 1 in 75 to a summit at Acrefair (0–66). Here the industrial branch from Trevor and the Pontcysyllte canal basin passed underneath. The descent was almost as steep, initially 1 in 85 to Trevor (1–64) and then 1 in 75 through Sun Bank (3–41) and most of the way to Llangollen (5–40). Trevor was the point at which traffic from the various brick, chemical and engineering works in the area was marshalled, with sidings for this purpose being provided on the south side of the line, just beyond the station. The simple halt at Sun Bank is significant in the line's history as the site of a tragic accident in September 1945 when the Chester–Barmouth mail train was derailed after the railway embankment had been washed away by the water from a four-mile stretch of the Llangollen Canal. Driver David Jones of Wrexham was killed and the railway was closed for almost a fortnight while recovery and rebuilding operations took place. On the descent to Llangollen, the railway and the River Dee converged until at the town's station a single road bridge crossed both and the proximity of the down platform to the river meant that the footbridge was built with the staircase cantilevered out over the river. The length of the platforms at Llangollen, with separate exits at the western end, highlight the former role of the railway in bringing many thousands of day trippers to the town and also serve as a reminder of the length of the summer Saturday holiday trains to Barmouth and other Cardigan Bay resorts.

Shortly after leaving the station, Llangollen Goods Junction (5–72) is reached. The signal box here marked the end of the double-track section from Llangollen Line Junction and also controlled access to the goods yard and Pentrefelin sidings. Llangollen Goods yard is located on the north side and higher than the line between the station and Goods Junction, while Pentrefelin sidings are on the same side of the line but at a lower level, between Goods Junction and the bridge over the River Dee. Both areas are now used by the Llangollen Railway for the storage and restoration of locomotives and rolling stock, but in previous times the goods yard would receive and dispatch a wide range of commodities, while excursion stock would be stabled at Pentrefelin.

Beyond the bridge the 1 in 100 climb which has prevailed since leaving Llangollen station steepens to 1 in 80 for the climb to Berwyn station and on to Berwyn tunnel. At Berwyn (7–06) the railway, Thomas Telford's Holyhead Road (today's A5) and the western extremity of the Llangollen Canal are all funnelled into the narrowing valley of the Dee and the river is itself crossed by two bridges – the Chain Bridge footbridge (after which the nearby hotel is named) and the road bridge, which carries the B5103 which links the A5 and the A542 Horsehoe Pass.

The builders of the line had little option but to tunnel through the northern extremity of the Berwyn Mountains. At 689-yards long, the tunnel is one of the longest single-bore railway tunnels in Britain. Through the tunnel the gradient eased to 1 in 135 and, on emerging from the western portal, levelled off. At this point the railway is well above the Dee. At Deeside (8–63), a passing loop was added in 1908 in order to break up the five mile section from Llangollen Goods Junction to Glyndyfrdwy (10–58), a facility which in practice was probably only used with any regularity on summer Saturdays. The present signal box at Deeside was built by the Llangollen Railway to a Cheshire Lines Committee design, in contrast with the Great Western Railway timber structure which was originally provided. Approaching Glyndyfrdwy on a sweeping reverse curve, there was a small goods yard to the south of the line where slate and slab brought down from the Moelfferna quarry on a narrow-gauge tramway was transhipped. A minor road is crossed at a gated level-crossing before the station is reached. Although perhaps giving the impression that it has always been there, with the exception of the original station building which survives as a private residence, much of the present station has been built from scratch since 1990. The signal box at the level crossing was originally at Leaton on the Shrewsbury–Chester line, the station building was previously an office at Northwich locomotive shed in Cheshire and the additional demonstration signal box at the west end was recovered from Barmouth South.

Beyond Glyndyfrdwy the line continues westwards, climbing almost imperceptibly to Carrog (12–67). Here once again the main station building is original but most of the other infrastructure is new construction by the Llangollen Railway. On the south of the line, a mile beyond Carrog, was Carrog Slate Siding, another transhipment point for slates quarried nearby. A little further on was Bonwm Halt (14–13), one of a number of simple platforms added by the Great Western Railway and often only served by request.

Approaching Corwen (15–50), the most extensive of all the intermediate stations, the Denbigh, Ruthin & Corwen Railway's line trailed in from the north after crossing the Dee on an substantial bridge. The extensive facilities provided at Corwen reflect its role as a junction between two railway companies, an arrangement which led in the mid 1920s to most staff being paid for jointly by the Great Western and the London, Midland & Scottish Railways, although the station master and half of one signalman were paid for solely by the Great Western. Corwen was also home to the Great Western's District Inspector who was responsible for the entire route from Llangollen Line Junction–Barmouth Junction and the Blaenau Ffestiniog and Pontcysyllte branches. In the early years of the line, the locomotive shed here provided much of the motive power required for workings to Ruabon, but this role declined during the early part of the twentieth century and the Great Western ceased to use it in 1927. Reflecting the railway's interests in other forms of transport, Corwen was also the base for a Great Western omnibus which operated to nearby villages and, on Sundays, to Llangollen where it connected with the limited train service provided to and from Ruabon.

Beyond Corwen, the line took a south-westerly course with stations serving the villages of Cynwyd (17–56), Llandrillo (20–32) and Llandderfel (23–08) before reaching Bala Junction (26–42). The line was never far from the river Dee and crossed it twice between Llandrillo and Llandderfel. The terrain on this section was far less severe than on most of the remainder of the route as, after a gentle climb at 1 in 200 over the two miles from Corwen to Cynwyd, it was effectively level for the following nine miles to Bala Junction. Apart from the two crossings of the Dee, the only other significant engineering feature is the 147-yard Llandderfel tunnel at Tŷ-tan-y-graig, between Llandderfel and Bala Junction. The great nineteenth century engineer and industrialist Henry Robertson owned two country houses, Crogen and Palé, close to the line. Crogen was served by a private halt between Llandrillo and Llandderfel, while visitors to Palé, including Queen Victoria in 1889, were met from Llandderfel.

When first built, Bala Junction station was inaccessible except by train, being provided solely for passengers to change to and from branch trains for Bala and Blaenau Ffestiniog. Subsequently, footpath access was provided, although even then the station only appeared in timetables in a footnote referenced from the Bala arrival and departure times. From south–north the layout consisted of the down platform, an island platform serving the up line and the branch and a passing loop (without a platform) used primarily to permit the locomotive of the branch train to run round the coaches. The branch was only accessible from the branch platform, which was also signalled to be accessible to main line trains in either direction.

Henry Robertson
Industrialist, engineer and railway pioneer, who resided at Palê Hall, Llandrillo .

Beyond Bala Junction the line continued south west alongside the southern shore of Llyn Tegid (Bala Lake) for most of the five miles to Llanuwchllyn (31–44). Two halts were added on this section by the Great Western: Bala Lake Halt (27–13) was opened in 1934, a short distance from the Junction, and on the site of the original Bala station (it is now the Bala terminus of the Bala Lake Railway, which is based at Llanuwchllyn) and a little over two miles further on is Llangower (29–37), opened as a halt in 1929 (now the midway point of the Bala Lake Railway, for which role it has been equipped with a new platform and a signalled passing loop). Half-a-mile further on was Flag Station (30–15), originally a private station provided for Sir Watkin Williams Wynn who lived at Glan Llyn on the opposite side of the lake. The unusual name was taken from the practice of passengers arriving at the halt raising a flag to summon the boatman to take them across the lake. In 1931, Flag Station became a public halt and in 1950 was renamed Glan Llyn.

Beyond Llanuwchllyn, the character of the line changed significantly as it passed to the north of Aran Fawddwy. The summit of the line was at Garneddwen (34–33), the culmination of a $2^{1}/_{2}$-mile climb at 1 in 63 from Llanuwchllyn. A passing loop was provided at Garneddwen in 1913 but, like Deeside, was not always in use. Short platforms were added in 1928, creating Garneddwen Halt. A halt was also opened at Llys (33–04), between Llanuwchllyn and Garneddwen, in 1934. From the summit at Garneddwen the line followed the valley of the River Wnion and descended steeply over the next $3^{1}/_{2}$ miles to Drws-y-Nant (37–61), another location where river, road and railway came together. The descent continued over the next $3^{1}/_{2}$ to Bontnewydd (41–36), with gradients as steep as 1 in 50. An intermediate halt, Wnion Halt (39–60), was added in 1933. Originally Bontnewydd only had a single platform, but a passing loop and second platform were added in 1923. The descent continued for a further 3 miles to Dolgellau, passing the short-lived Dolserau Halt (for Torrent Walk) (42–40), which was only open between 1935 and 1951.

Dolgellau (44–36) marked the end of the descent from the summit at Garneddwen and another change in the character of the line, as the remainder of the route to Barmouth Junction was effectively level. Extensive facilities were provided at Dolgellau for passengers and goods, including goods shed, cattle pens and a small petrol depot, reflecting its status as the county town of Merionethshire and, in railway terms, up to 1922, the junction between the Great Western and Cambrian Railways. A small turntable allowed locomotives to be turned although there was no shed – that was 2 miles further on at Penmaenpool (46–52) where the station was adjacent to the southern end of the toll bridge over the Mawddach. Beyond Penmaenpool there was a short siding at Garth where traffic from Ty'n-y-coed quarry was loaded. On the opposite side of the line at this point, the

Cambrian Railways provided two cottages for members of their engineering staff. At Arthog (51–18) the station only ever consisted of a timber platform and waiting shelter, with a single siding for goods traffic. Some impression of the character of this part of the line may be obtained from a Great Western Railway internal report which described the 7 miles from Penmaenpool through Arthog to Barmouth Junction as 'one of the most enchanting in the world, giving views of sea, river and mountains.'

The layout at Barmouth Junction (52–18) reflects the evolution of the railways in the immediate area. The first section to be used was the south–east curve, for trains from Tywyn working through to Penmaenpool, from July 1865. Services on the main coast line, across the estuary, began in July 1867. The east–north curve opened at the same time, thus allowing trains from Penmaenpool to run through to Barmouth.

Barmouth Bridge is perhaps one of the most iconic engineering features on Britain's railways. From the south, the present bridge consists of a timber approach viaduct of 113 spans leading to an opening section at the north end. Originally this was of a sliding drawbridge design, but was replaced in 1899 by the present swinging section, albeit one which has been locked closed for many years.

Barmouth station (53–62 from Llangollen Line Junction and 54–36 from Ruabon station) occupies a prime location close to the seafront. The majority of the station is located north of the level crossing, formerly controlled by the South signal box, although south of the crossing was a separate bay platform which enabled originating and terminating services to operate without obstructing the level crossing or opening the North box.

1. RUABON, 1959
Ex GWR 4-4-0 Dukedogs, Nº. 9018 and 9004, wait to leave Ruabon with a Ffestiniog Railway Society special bound for Porthmadog. The train had been hauled from London (Paddington) by Castle class 4-6-0, Nº. 5069, *Isambard Kingdom Brunel*. 18 April 1959. [Authors' Collection]

2. RUABON, *c*.1910
Ruabon once boasted a staff of over 60 and a good number of whom are seen in this early postcard view, with the station bookstall prominent in the foreground. By contrast, the present-day station has been reduced to unstaffed status with waiting shelters.   [Lens of Sutton]

3. RUABON, 1957
A view of the southern end of the station with the large nameboard listing the main stations on the Barmouth line. An ex Great Western Railway 2-6-0 Mogul is shunting the yard with Ruabon Middle signal box on the left and locomotive turntable on the right. 12 August 1957. [Hugh Davies/'Photos from the Fifties']

4. RUABON, 1960s
British Railways Standard Class 4, N⁰· 75020, stands in the bay platform with a service for Barmouth.
[Lens of Sutton]

5. RUABON, 1961
Pannier tank N⁰· 4645 draws admiring looks from two young fans as it waits to depart with the final passenger train for Blaenau Ffestiniog. This special train was arranged by the Stephenson Locomotive Society to mark the closure of the Bala–Blaenau Ffestiniog line, 22 January 1961.
[Late B.J. Dobbs]

20 *Rails Through Bala*

6. RUABON, 1965
Ex LMS Black Five 4-6-0, Nº. 45256, passes over Llangollen Line Junction with a freight train bound for Chester during the winter of 1965. The line to Barmouth had closed to passengers on 15 January 1965 but remained open for freight as far as Llangollen. [A.O. Wynn]

7. RUABON, 1964
A Talyllyn AGM Special takes the Barmouth line at Llangollen Line Junction, hauled by No. 7827 *Lydham Manor* and recently preserved Prairie tank No. 4555. 26 September 1964. [E. N. Kneale]

8. ACREFAIR, 1950s
A view looking towards Llangollen showing the signal box and the building on the down platform.
[Lens of Sutton]

9. ACREFAIR, 1950s
A view of Acrefair station and its small goods yard, which is full of vans. A passenger train waits to leave for Ruabon, while the factory on the right is the Air Products site; closed in 2009. [Denbighshire Record Office]

Rails Through Bala 23

10. ACREFAIR, *c.*1900
An old postcard view showing the bridge carrying the railway over the Llangollen road in Acrefair village. [Arthur Jones]

11. ACREFAIR, 1965
This picture shows the freight line in Acrefair, which left the main line at Trevor Yard and went via Legacy to serve several industrial locations. 5 June 1965. [C.H.A. Townley]

12. TREVOR, 1935
GWR 0-6-0ST, N⁰ 2135, is shunting a 'Toad' brake van in Trevor yard in this early view. Worthy of note is the ornate gas lamp. [Kidderminster Railway Museum]

13. TREVOR, *c*.1965
A good view of Trevor station showing the waiting shelter on the up platform and the main building on the down platform. The train crew on the down platform have probably been taking a break before returning to their pannier tank in the yard. The two young boys watching them are no doubt hoping to be invited onto the footplate.
[P.E. Baughan]

Rails Through Bala 25

14. TREVOR, *c.*1966
Trevor signal box stands sentinel as a pannier tank shunts the daily trip freight in Trevor yard. After the end of passenger services in 1965, this Wrexham–Llangollen freight was the only traffic on the line. [Brian Taylor]

15. SUN BANK, 1955
On a sunny summer day, pannier tank, N[o.] 6420, propels a two-coach auto train towards Wrexham. 6 August 1955. [R.W. Hinton]

26 *Rails Through Bala*

16. SUN BANK, 1945

On 7 September 1945, the canal bank collapsed and a section of track was washed away. The telegraph wires remained intact, allowing the signalman at Trevor to send the 3.55 a.m. Chester–Barmouth mail train into the section, where it ran into the breach. The driver was killed, but the fireman and guard survived. [Authors' Collection]

17. SUN BANK, 1955
An old postcard provides a rare view of Sun Bank Halt. It also shows clearly the proximity of canal and railway. [John Ryan Collection]

18. LLANGOLLEN, 1957
A view looking towards Ruabon with Mogul 2-6-0, N⁰· 6357, heading a four-coach train for Barmouth. [C.L. Caddy]

19. LLANGOLLEN, c.1960
This photograph has been taken from the road bridge (seen behind the train in the previous photograph) as an enthusiasts' railtour approaches Llangollen with 0-6-0 pannier tank, N$^{o.}$ 4683, in charge of seven brake vans.
[Authors' Collection]

20. LLANGOLLEN, c.1890
An early view of Llangollen station, prior to construction of the footbridge. The small wooden signal-box was subsequently replaced by a brick-built structure and the platforms lengthened to accommodate excursion traffic.
[Denbighshire Record Office]

21. LLANGOLLEN, *c*.1898
An 0-6-0 saddle tank stands on the up line at Llangollen station with what appears to be an engineers' train. In view of the large number of staff invovled, it is possible the work was in connection with the doubling of the line from Ruabon. [Mr Scott Archer Collection]

22. LLANGOLLEN, *c*.1960
A detailed view of Llangollen station, which clearly shows how it was squeezed into a small space between the river and the town. The brick signal box and cantilever footbridge are shown to good effect. [E.N. Kneale]

23. LLANGOLLEN, *c*.1958
Looking towards Corwen, with the telegraph pole route prominent on the left of the picture and the horse landing stage on the right. [Stephenson Locomotive Society]

24. LLANGOLLEN GOODS JUNCTION, 1950s
An auto train is seen at Goods Junction heading towards Llangollen station, probably with a Bala Junction–Wrexham working. The track layout here was quite complicated. In addition to the double-track main line, the line going off diagonally to the right led to the goods yard while the line to the right of the auto train provided a direct connection between the goods yard and Penrefelin sidings. The main line became single track beyond this point. [C.E. Stephens]

25. LLANGOLLEN GOODS JUNCTION, 1967

Former LMSR Class 8F, No. 48697, stands at Llangollen Goods Junction waiting to run round an enthusiasts' railtour, which was visiting the line. This tour was the last passenger train to visit the line and was not permitted to stop at Llangollen station because the BR management at the time had concerns that if it did it would add weight to the arguements of campaigners proposing that special trains should be run to Llangollen for the International Musical Eisteddfod. 29 April 1967. [Brian Taylor]

26. PENTREFELIN SIDINGS, 1950s

BR Standard Class 4, No. 75002, at the head of a van train for Cuthbert's Seeds waits to leave Pentrefelin sidings. These sidings used to serve a slate mill, via an interchange siding and an inclined tramway, but from the 1950s they were used for stabling stock from excursion trains visiting the Llangollen International Eisteddfod.
[Llangollen Railway Archives]

27. BERWYN, 1910
A postcard view showing the station alongside the River Dee. The road bridge passed under the railway and over the river and was known as King's Bridge. The signal was controlled by station staff to stop trains when they had passengers wishing to board.   [Authors' Collection]

28. BERWYN, 1869
An artist's impression of Berwyn station taken from an early postcard.   [Authors' Collection]

29. BERWYN, c.1955
Pannier tank, Nº 9763, pauses at Berwyn with a stopping train. Note how the platform had been extended onto the viaduct to accommodate longer trains. [Alan Donaldson]

30. DEESIDE LOOP, 1963
Shortly after leaving Berwyn, westbound trains arrived at Deeside, a crossing loop and signal box installed in 1908. This was to provide an additional passing facility, particularly on busy summer Saturdays. The box was a standard GWR timber-built type, with 18 levers and a switch to enable it to close at less busy times. [H.J. Leadbetter]

31. GLYNDYFRDWY, *c*.1900
A postcard view looking towards Corwen, showing the main station building on the down platform and the shelter and signal box on the up platform. [Lens of Sutton]

32. GLYNDYFRDWY, *c*.1900
Another early postcard view looking towards the Llantisilio Mountains. The generous proportions of the station building are well illustrated in this view. [Lens of Sutton]

33. GLYNDYFRDWY, *c*.1958
The signal box is prominent in this later view with a pannier tank and two coaches on a stopping train for Wrexham.   [G. Baxter]

34. GLYNDYFRDWY TRAMWAY, 1930s
Looking down the inclined tramway which connected a slate quarry with an interchange siding at Glyndyfrdwy, passing under the A5 road to reach the valley floor.   [J. Ryan Collection]

35. CARROG, 1915
In February 1915 the embankment at Glyndŵr's Mount near Carrog, slipped across the railway and into the river. In an era when labour was plentiful, a large gang of men with picks and shovels are seen carrying out remedial work to stabilise the bank. [Authors' Collection]

36. CARROG, 1950s
Carrog had a substantial stone-built station building on the up side provided by the original company. The signal box on the up side and the waiting room on the down side, which is just out of view, were built by the GWR. [Lens of Sutton]

37. CARROG, *c.*1950s
The sign on the A5 road pointing to Carrog station still refers to the Great Western Railway and several enamel advertising signs are shown in this street scene.
[Hugh Davies/'Photos from the Fifties']

38. CARROG, *c.*1950s
Before the era of foreign travel and package holidays, old railway coaches were converted to camping coaches and hired out for family holidays. One such elderly coach is seen in the sidings at Carrog with a family in residence. [Hugh Davies/'Photos from the Fifties']

39. CARROG, 1950s
Prairie tank Nº 4102 heads a four-coach train towards Llangollen. The signal box required substantial rebuilding when the preservation society took over.
[Hugh Davies/'Photos from the Fifties']

40. BONWM HALT, 1960s
Typical of many of the halts on the line was this one at Bonwm, between Carrog and Corwen, adjacent to the main A5 road. Increasing road competition was the main reason for the demise of traffic on the line and the loaded Crosville bus says it all. [Lens of Sutton]

41. BONWM HALT, 1960s
A view of Bonwm from the road showing the wooden waiting shelter and name boards. [Lens of Sutton]

42. CORWEN, 1947
A former London & North Western Railway 2-4-2-tank loco in Corwen at the head of a train it has worked from Denbigh. Prominent on the right of the photograph is the railway delivery lorry standing against the corrugated iron shed. [P.B. Whitehouse]

43. CORWEN, 1957
6 August 1957. An aerial view of the Dee valley showing the junction between the ex GWR and LNWR routes: the LNWR coming from the left and crossing the Dee on a substantial bridge, while the GWR follows the Dee valley. The platforms of Corwen station are just visible at the lower right. [Aerofilms]

44. CORWEN, *c.*1910
Corwen, in pre-grouping days, with its distinctive canopy and station bookstall. The extensive goods yard is visible beyond the footbridge, while a number of railway employees pose on the platform. [Lens of Sutton]

45. CORWEN, *c.*1910
A period view, showing the kind of freight traffic the line used to handle, as an open-cab GWR 0-6-0 saddle tank brings a substantial timber train into the yard. Also evident is the A5 road bridge to the rear of the train, and the siding used for coaling locomotives heading towards the signal box. A crane for this purpose can be seen behind the box. [Authors' Collection]

Rails Through Bala 41

46. CORWEN, *c.*1930
Another GWR 0-6-0 saddle tank, Nº 772, stands in the up platform at Corwen with a rake of clerestory coaches. [Authors' Collection]

47. CORWEN, 1963
A Tallyllyn Railway special train hauled by two Manor-class locos (Nº 7827 *Lydham Manor* and Nº 7822 *Foxcote Manor*) waits to depart for Towyn. 29 September 1963. [E.C. Lloyd]

48. CORWEN, *c*.1960s
DMUs were only occasional visitors to the line, this one being used for an enthusiasts' special which had arrived at Corwen via the Denbigh line.   [C.L. Caddy Collection]

49. CORWEN, 1964
The frontage of the main station building with its two imposing gables and central canopy. As well as the usual booking hall and ladies' and gents' lavatories, there was also a refreshment room, porters' room and waiting room. [H.J. Leadbetter]

50. CORWEN, 1964
The goods yard as seen from the platform end, with the cattle dock and goods shed to the left and goods loops to the right. In the distance is the water tank that supplied the loco shed. [H.J. Leadbetter]

51. CORWEN, 1961
The West end of the Corwen layout with signal box on the right and water tower and turntable on the left. In the centre of the photograph, almost lost in the grass, is a disused loco inspection pit. This was originally covered by a shed, which closed during the 1930s. 28 May 1961. [R.S. Carpenter]

52. CORWEN, 1963
Pannier tank N⁰· 4683 passes Corwen West signal box with the 5.40 p.m. Bala–Wrexham train. The shed on the right was for dealing with agricultural goods. 5 October 1963.   [M. Mensing]

53. CYNWYD, *c*.1910
In an effort to reduce operating costs steam railmotors were tried on the Wrexham–Bala trains for a short period and N⁰· 9 is seen posed at Cynwyd with the station staff and members of the public. The Great Western Society, based at Didcot, commissioned the reconstruction of a replica steam railmotor and much of the work has been carried out in the workshops at Llangollen. Successful test/demonstration running was carried out between Llangollen and Carrog in the spring of 2011. [Lens of Sutton]

54. CYNWYD, 1962
Pannier tank, No. 3749, has just three passengers to pick up at Cynwyd as it arrives with a four-coach train in the summer of 1962. 2 August 1962.   [H.B. Priestley/Pacer Archives]

55. LLANDRILLO, c.1910
An early postcard view of Llandrillo, complete with porter's trolley on the up platform, whilst members of the station staff pose near the signal box. [Lens of Sutton]

56. LLANDRILLO, 1960s
Llandrillo Station, 21 miles 2 chains from Ruabon , basking peacefully in the sun and looking a little unkempt, was situated about ³/₄ mile from the villages it purported to serve. Traffic was sparse, although goods traffic was once an important source of revenue here.   [Authors' Collection]

57. LLANDRILLO, 1965
After closure, the buildings remained intact, although boarded up against vandals. The solitary sheep on the platform is probably grateful for the fact that there is no train to take her to market.   [H.J. Leadbetter]

Rails Through Bala 47

58. CROGEN HALL HALT, *c*.1965
Crogen Hall Halt, between Llandrillo and Llanderfel, was a private halt provided for a local landowner in the 1920s. The halt was only open for a short period and was of single-coach length. This picture was probably taken shortly after the closure of the line. [Lens of Sutton]

59. LLANDERFEL, *c*.1910
Prospective passengers pose for the camera on a rather damp day at Llanderfel. While the up platform had the main station building and signal box, the down had just a waiting shelter and on this occasion, a single passenger. [Lens of Sutton]

60. LLANDDERFEL, c.1950
Pannier tank Nº 6406, working in auto mode on a Bala-Wrexham train, is crossing a down train hauled by an ex GWR Mogul. The signalman can be seen walking along the platform with the token for the down train over his arm. [Authors' Collection]

61. LLANDDERFEL, 1950s
An Ivatt 2-6-0, Nº 46470, often affectionately referred to as the 'Mickey Mouse' type, arrives at Llanderfel with a two-coach train while the signalman prepares to exchange the single line tokens. [J. Roberts Collection]

Rails Through Bala 49

62. LLANDDERFEL, 1964
On the night of 13/14 December 1964, the line between Llandderfel and Llandrillo was subjected to severe flooding and the resultant damage is shown dramatically in this photograph.   [R. Icke]

63. BALA JUNCTION, 1955
A general view of Bala Junction, showing the island platform, signal box and footbridge. 16 April 1955.
[H.B. Priestley/Pacer Archives collection]

64. BALA JUNCTION, 1959
Pannier tank N⁰· 8727 on the single-coach shuttle to Bala town stands alongside classmate N⁰· 8691, which is adjacent to the signal box. 3 April 1959. [J.A. Peden]

65. BALA JUNCTION, 1950s
0-4-2T, N⁰· 5811, stands at the down platform with a train for Dollgellau. An unidentified pannier is at the island platform with the Bala Town shuttle. [Lens of Sutton]

66. BALA JUNCTION, 1963
Snow blankets everything in this wintry view of Bala Junction, taken from a departing Dollgellau-bound train. [H.J. Leadbetter]

67. BALA JUNCTION, 1953
Pannier tank Nº 7443 is caught at the east end of Bala Junction during a run round manoeuvre. Alongside the loco are two classic wooden post signals. 15 August 1953. [H.C. Casserley]

68. BALA JUNCTION, 1960s
The Bala Town shuttle departs behind a BR 84xxx tank, while the signalman looks on from his open window. Also prominent are the bracket signal and station nameboard, advising passengers to change here for Bala.
[Dave Southern Collection]

69. BALA JUNCTION, 1950s
Ex-GWR Mogul, N° 6311, entering Bala Junction with a lengthy freight train. It has used the freight relief line for the journey from Bala.   [C.L. Caddy Collection]

Rails Through Bala 53

70. BALA JUNCTION, 1959
As pannier N⁰ 8727 waits at the island platform with the Bala Town shuttle the signalman walks down the box steps to hand over the token. 3 April 1959.   [J.A. Peden]

71. BALA JUNCTION, 1963
The main station building was located on the island platform and served both the branch and main line. While one could buy tickets here, it existed mainly as an interchange between the two lines and the only access was by a ½-mile long footpath from the nearest road. [H.J. Leadbetter]

54 *Rails Through Bala*

72. BALA JUNCTION, 1961
The final train to Blaenau Ffestiniog, hauled by pannier tanks N°s. 4645 and 8971, approaches the island platform at Bala Junction. 22 January 1961.
[Late B.J. Dobbs]

73. BALA JUNCTION, 1961
Another view of the last train as it takes the curve onto the branch heading for Bala and Blaenau Ffestiniog. 22 January 1961.
[E.N. Bellass]

74. BALA JUNCTION, 1950s
Mogul 2-6-0, Nº 5344, carrying express-code headlamps, arrives at Bala Junction with a Chester-bound train of chocolate and cream coaches. [A. Donaldson]

75. NEAR BALA LAKE HALT, 1960s
Another Mogul 2-6-0, No. 7341, runs along the edge of Bala Lake, between Llangower Halt and Bala Lake Halt, with a train for Chester.
[Late Derek Cross]

76. BALA LAKE HALT, 1960s
A view of Bala Lake Halt, which was a coach-length long and comprised a waiting shelter, lamp standard and nameboard, was located near the road at the Bala end of the lake.   [C.L. Caddy]

77. LLANGOWER HALT, *c.*1964
Llangower Halt opened to serve the small village of Llangower by Bala Lake, comprised a single-coach platform with a nameboard, waiting shelter and lamp, with access by public footpath. [C.L. Caddy]

78. GLAN LLYN (FLAG) HALT, c.1964
Glan Llyn Halt was originally a flag station, built for local landowner, Sir Watkin Williams Wynn. The platform, viewed from the Bala end, comprised a wooden waiting shelter split in two, one side being open and the other a lock up with a corrugated iron roof. There was also a lamp and station name board.   [C.L. Caddy]

79. LLANUWCHLLYN, 1963
Although there is only a small amount of snow in evidence, the snowplough-fitted pannier tank passing the signalbox is a sure sign that more can be expected.   [J. Roberts Collection]

80. LLANUWCHLLYN, 1959
A short freight train leaves under clear signals, passing the goods loop with the loading gauge and warehouse alongside, and a siding with a cattle dock. At the start of the down platform is a lamp hut and token catcher. 10 April 1959.   [H.B. Priestley/Pacer Archive Collection]

81. LLANUWCHLLYN, 1962
BR Standard 4-6-0, No. 75006, makes ready to leave with a four-coach train for Chester in August 1962. Note the token catcher on the down side, in front of the lamp hut, and the old style round point rodding in the foreground. [C.L. Caddy]

82. LLANUWCHLLYN, 1962
A view looking towards Dolgellau. Another water tower can be seen, this location obviously having a useful water source. Beyond the platform end is the brick-built hut provided for the permanent way gang.   [P.J. Garland]

83. LLANUWCHLLYN, 1962
Llanuwchlllyn, showing the main station building and signal box and conical water tower on the up platform and the brick-built, slate-roofed waiting room on the down side. Note the vintage porters' trolleys on the up platform. 25 August 1962.   [P.J. Garland]

84. LLYS HALT, 1950s
Llys Halt was a single platform located on the down side of the line, with a platform 70-feet long. The halt comprised a timber-faced platform with ash backfill and surface, with a waiting shelter, name board and paraffin lamp for lighting. Access was via the farm crossing in the foreground.   [R.S. Carpenter Collection]

85. GARNEDDWEN, *c*.1964
The primary role of the signalbox at Garneddwen, like the one at Deeside, was to provide another passing place for the havy trains provided on summer Saturdays to convey holiday makers to the coastal resorts. A halt was also provided at a later date. In this view, probably taken after the London Midland region took responsibility fr the line, the loop was closed and the nameboard has been displaced. Note the staggered platforms.   [Lens of Sutton]

86. GARNEDDWEN, 1950s
From a cameraman noted for his atmospheric views comes this typical three-coach local train, hauled by one of the ubiquitous Moguls.
[Late Derek Cross]

87. GARNEDDWEN, 1960s
A closer view of the signalbox and token exchange equipment, taken from a passing train. [E. Frangleton]

88. DRWS-Y-NANT, 1950s
The auditor pays a visit when porter/signalman Davies and Station Master Ellis are on duty. [J. Roberts Collection]

89. DRWS-Y-NANT, 1964

BR Standard 4, 4-6-0, No. 75026, passes a light engine at Drws-y-Nant with a Wrexham-bound train on a summer Saturday in 1964. Note the cant on the line at this point. [Hugh Davies/'Photos from the Fifties']

90. DRWS-Y-NANT, 1965
A view looking towards Dolgellau, showing the end of the loop with the token catcher on the up side, with a screen behind it to prevent a misplaced token falling into the river! On the left is the goods siding with cattle dock, loading gauge and lamp hut in the yard. The yard can be seen to be accessed by some very tight pointwork.
[H.J. Leadbetter]

91. DRWS-Y-NANT, 1965
A closer view of the token catcher with its protective screen. [H.J. Leadbetter]

66 *Rails Through Bala*

92. DRWS-Y-NANT, 1965
A view looking towards the Dolgellau end, with the signal box on the down platform, the crossing gates over the minor road and a store shed on the end of the up platform. The topography here brought together the railway, river and adjacent main road in close proximity to each other.   [H.J. Leadbetter]

93. DRWS-Y-NANT, 1965
The main station building, seen on the down platform, comprised booking office, ladies' and gents' WCs and waiting room.   [H.J. Leadbetter]

94. DRWS-Y-NANT, 1950s
The signalman waits on the platform by the store shed ready to receive the token from the fireman on a Wrexham-bound train headed by a Mogul 2-6-0, while in the loop a down train waits bound for Barmouth.
[Authors' Collection]

95. NEAR WNION HALT, 1961
BR Standard 4-6-0, Nº 75054, heads the *Welsh Chieftain* Land Cruise train on 1 September 1961 beside the river Wnion, between Drws-y-Nant and Bontnewydd. The *Welsh Chieftain* Land Cruise train was one of a number of special trains for tourists run from Rhyl, via Denbigh and Corwen, to Barmouth and back, via Afon Wen and Caernarfon.   [E.N. Bellass]

96. WNION HALT, 1960s
Wnion Halt was located on the up side and comprised a single 70-foot timber-faced platform with a gravel surface. Access was by footpath located behind the halt to the road. [Lens of Sutton]

97. BONTNEWYDD, 1960s
Ivatt 2-6-0, N°· 46446, enters the loop with a four-coach train bound for Barmouth. The extension to the down platform backs on to the riverbank. [M. Jenkins]

98. BONTNEWYDD, 1950s
A general view with a small boy standing by the main station building and goods shed on the up-side platform. At the far end we see the crossing gates for the minor road and the signal box, located at the end of the down platform. This platform was added when a passing loop was put in after 1923 and was of timber construction. Note also the corrugated-iron waiting shelter.   [H.B. Priestley/Pacer Archive collection]

99. BONTNEWYDD, *c.*1910
A pre-1923 view, before the passing loop was installed. Th uniformed man standing in front of the original wooden-built station is probably the station master. The men standing on the track are presumed to be the local permanent way gang, differently attired to those affected by today's Health & Safety legislation.   [J. Roberts Collection]

70 *Rails Through Bala*

100. DOLSERAU HALT, *c*.1950s
Dolserau Halt was a small platform on the down side of the line, with a sleeper facing and a gravel surface. A solitary passenger waits in the shelter while the name board advertises a well-known walk to the nearby river. [LGRP]

101. DOLGELLEU, 1961
Mogul 2-6-0, N°· 6339, runs into Dolgelleu with a Ruabon–Pwllheli train in May 1961. Note also, on the up platform, the water tower and wooden bracket signal and, on the down side, the old camping coach located behind the signal box.   [J.R. Besley]

102. DOLGELLEY, c.1890s
A posed photograph taken in the yard at Dolgellau with GWR open-back saddle tank, Nº 1515. The engineman on the footplate appears to be holding the train staff and the presence of the workforce suggests this is probably a 'Possession' for engineering works. [J. Roberts Collection]

103. DOLGELLAU, 1963
As a down train arrives at Dolgellau, the fireman and signalman prepare to exchange tokens from the signal box. Note the trackless 42-foot turntable, showing evidence of when Dolgellau was a terminal station for services from Barmouth and engines, latterly in the form of a pannier tanks or 14xxs, were turned.   [H.J. Leadbetter]

104. DOLGELLEY, 1950s
Mogul 2-6-0, Nº 6316, heads a five-coach train through Dolgelley bound for Wrexham. Note the disused signal box with all functions transferred to the signal box built at the Bala end of the down platform.   [E.E. Smith]

105. DOLGELLEY, *c.*1900
A vintage train of Cambrian 4-wheel and 6-wheel coaches headed by a 2-4-0T passes the goods-yard warehouse on the approach to Dolgelley station. Note also the group of locals enjoying the sun on the riverbank, which runs in front of the railway at this point. [National Library of Wales]

106. DOLGELLAU, 1964
Stationmaster Edwards stands on the platform at Dolgellau with the train staff, 12 December 1964. The floodwater caused the premature closure of the line which was scheduled to close 15 January 1965. [J. Roberts Collection]

107. DOLGELLAU, 1960s
The signalman on duty inside Dolgellau signal box in the 1960s. Note the old-style telephones, together with the special control instrument, permitting the release of tokens for track maintenance. [Authors' Collection]

108. DOLGELLAU, 1960
The station is about to have its third change of name. It was Dolgely until 1896 and was changed from Dolgelley to Dolgellau in 1960. The station staff stand in front of the Great Western Railway-style sign with raised metal letters on wood, while the new one is the standard BR enamel. [E. Frangleton]

Rails Through Bala 75

109. DOLGELLAU, 1960

A useful view of the station buildings, which illustrates their history. Middle left are the gabled stone buildings of the Bala & Dolgely Railway, extended (near left) by the GWR with a single-storey brick structure. On the right is the Cambrian Railways building, this location being an end-on junction. The original signalbox can just be seen beyond the footbridge, replaced by the GWR box beyond the right-hand platform. [Lens of Sutton]

110. DOLGELLEY, 1960
In 1960 a mineral train leaves the goods yard at Dolgelley behind Mogul 2-6-0, N⁰· 5399, and onto the main line through the station. The goods train may call at other stations along the line, eventually finishing up at Croes Newydd marshalling yard, Wrexham. This view just pre-dates the change of nameboard. [E. Frangleton]

111. PENMAENPOOL, 1963
The station building, with a booking office, waiting area and stationmaster's house, was located by the road crossing. Beyond the George Hotel can be seen the locomotive shed. [H.J. Leadbetter]

112. PENMAENPOOL, 1960s
A view from the Barmouth end showing the end of the loop, the toll house for the bridge, signal box, train in the loop and the two sidings, one with a wagon in it by the goods shed.   [M. Jenkins]

113. PENMAENPOOL, 1962
BR Standard 4-6-0, N⁰· 75006, crosses the road at the end of the platform at Penmaenpool with a Wrexham train in 1962. On the wooden platform, with concrete supports, stands the signalman ready to exchange tokens. Note also the signal box and the wooden bridge crossing the river. [C.L. Caddy]

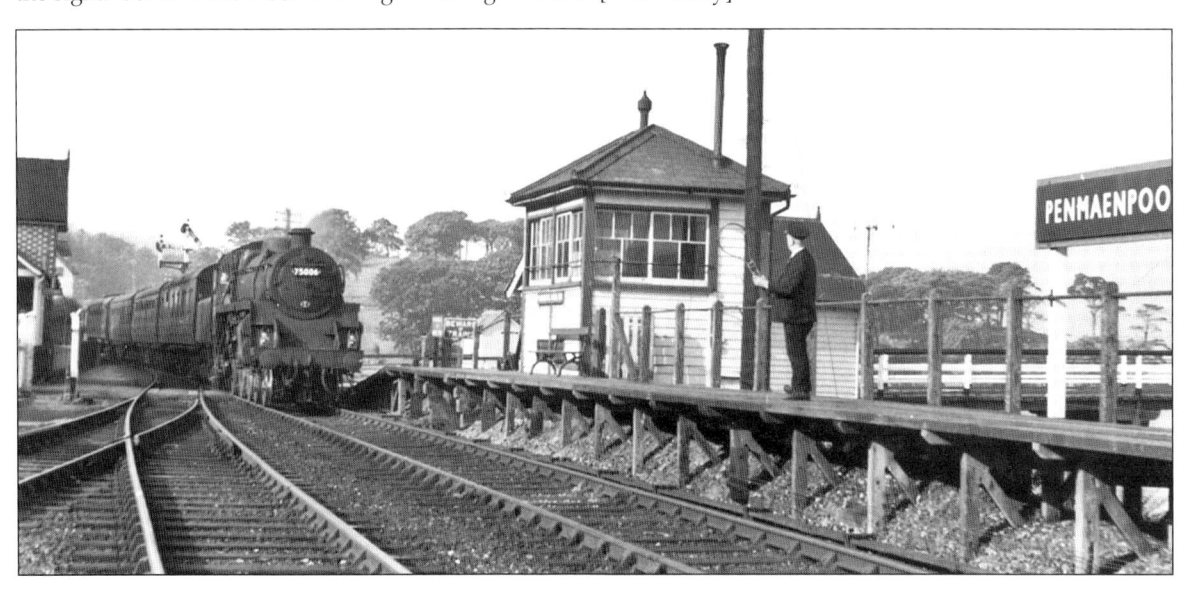

114. PENMAENPOOL SHED, 1963
Penmaenpool shed was opened by the Cambrian Railways in 1869 and provided engines for the Barmouth–Dolgellau service and banking or pilot engines for the summer Saturday services to the coast. On shed we see Ivatt 2-6-0, No. 46421, and BR Standard 4-6-0, No. 75029, awaiting the next turn of duty. Note the closeness of the main line passing the shed.   [C.L. Caddy]

115. PENMAENPOOL SHED, 1938
Great Western Railway engine No. 2279 and an unidentified sister engine stand just outside the shed. Note the store shed on the left and the fire irons leaning against the fence. 22 June 1938.   [Authors' Collection]

116 . PENMAENPOOL, 1950s
Ex GWR Mogul 2-6-0, Nº 7341, arrives under clear signals. The track here was on a raised embankment above a marshy area, which was tidal at this point. This is believed to be the same train previously illustrated near Garneddwen. [Late D. Cross]

117. ARTHOG, 1957
Ex GWR Manor 4-6-0, N⁰· 7817, arrives on the 16 August 1957 with a train for Wrexham. Note the station building with the corrugated iron roof, the fire buckets and the wooden platform on supports. There was no passing place here, but a siding was provided (controlled by a ground frame) which was the 'home' of a camping coach for a number of years.   [H.B. Priestley/Pacer Archive collection]

118. ARTHOG, 1950s
Ex GWR 0-4-2, N⁰· 1434, arrives with the auto train service between Barmouth and Dolgellau The engine is standing on a bridge, which is a cattle creep.   [Hugh Davies/'Photos from the Fifties']

119. MORFA MAWDDACH, 1961
Morfa Mawddach main station buildings situated in the 'V' of the coast line and the Ruabon line. As well as the usual facilities of booking hall, waiting room, ladies' and gents' WCs, the station also boasted a licensed refreshment room, believed to have been used by local residents as well as rail passengers. 29 September 1961.   [R.F. Roberts]

120. MORFA MAWDDACH, 1963
A BR Standard Class 4-6-0, N$^o.$ 75023, runs in with a train from the Ruabon line. Note the camping coach on the right behind the nameboard. These were a feature of many country stations in days gone by.   [C.L. Caddy]

121. MORFA MAWDDACH, 1961

Ex GWR Mogul 2-6-0, N° 7339, heads the 10.20 a.m. Barmouth–Birkenhead train into Morfa Mawddach, collecting the token from the signalman on the platform. 29 September 1961. [R.F. Roberts]

122. MORFA MAWDDACH, 1963
In 1960, British Railways agreed to change the name for Barmouth Junction station to Morfa Mawddach. The Welsh word *'morfa'* translates as 'salt marsh', evidence of which can be clearly seen in this photograph. Another BR Standard Class 4, No. 75006, arrives having just crossed the viaduct over the Mawddach estuary. There was a connecting spur at the back of the station, making it a triangular junction, which enabled tender engines terminating at Barmouth to be turned for their return journey. [B.J. Ashworth]

84 Rails Through Bala

123. BARMOUTH JUNCTION, 1940s
Believed to be a pre-nationalisation view of a Great Western Railway Mogul 2-6-0 taking the Ruabon road with a single coach train. Of note is the nameboard advising passengers on the former Cambrian line to change here for Llangollen, Ruabon and Chester.   [Late B.J. Dobbs]

124. BARMOUTH JUNCTION, 1950s
A general view of the approach to Barmouth Junction from the bridge end showing the signal box on the left, the main station buildings in the centre and the waiting shelter on the down side for the Coast line.
[Authors' Collection]

125. BARMOUTH BRIDGE, 1950s
An ex GWR 0-6-0, Nº 3213, with a passenger train, crosses over the section that swings round to allow the passage of boats up the Mawddach Estuary on their way to Barmouth. [Late D. Cross]

126. BARMOUTH BRIDGE, *c.*1900
A very early, rather indistinct view of the original lifting bridge and toll house for foot passengers using the footpath built alongside the railway bridge. [Authors' Collection]

127. BARMOUTH BRIDGE, 1950s
Ex GWR 0-6-0-tender engine, N⁰· 2202, comes off the bridge with a short train of coal wagons for distribution along the coast to various stations. Note also the wooden bridge the engine is crossing which gives access to a boathouse via a slipway. [Late D. Cross]

Rails Through Bala 87

128. BARMOUTH BRIDGE, *c*.1960
A rare view of the bridge being opened at Barmouth, possibly for river traffic but more likely a maintenance check. Note the safety boat moored underneath the bridge in case of mishap. [C.L. Caddy]

129. BARMOUTH, 1960s
BR Standard 2-6-2T, N⁰· 82000, comes over the concrete bridge by Barmouth harbour with a train of coal wagons and a Great Western 'Toad' brake van at the rear. [C.L. Caddy]

88 Rails Through Bala

130. BARMOUTH, 1920s
An unidentified GWR 2-4-0 leaves over the road crossing with a train of clerestory coaches passing the bay platform on the right. The rolling stock appears to be in the 'brownish lake'-livery used in the early years of the twentieth century.   [Lens of Sutton]

131. BARMOUTH, 1925
A vintage Great Western 2-4-0 stands in the bay platform with a service to Dolgellau on 15 June 1925. The rolling stock of a 6-wheel brake van and carriage of similar vintage is of note. [Lens of Sutton]

Rails Through Bala 89

132. BARMOUTH, 1963
BR Standard 4-6-0, Nº. 75009, backs onto its train over the road crossing in the centre of the town, protected by the signal box, to work the 2.35 p.m. to Birkenhead, 1 May 1963. The signal box is preserved on the Llangollen Railway and is now located at Glyndfrdwy. [R.F. Roberts]

133. BARMOUTH, 1950s
A view of Barmouth station showing the main Cambrian Railways buildings and the main through-platforms. There was another bay platform, with carriage sidings, just to the right of the photograph.
[Lens of Sutton]

134. BARMOUTH, 1950s
Ex Great Western Railway 4-6-0, N°· 7819, *Hinton Manor*, rests in the headshunt. The bay platform was mainly used for the short service to Dolgellau and excursion trains. This locomotive is now resident on the Severn Valley Railway. [Lens of Sutton]

Historical background: Bala–Blaenau Ffestiniog

As previously noted, the railway reached Bala from Llandrillo in April 1868 and opened onwards to Dolgellau four months later. The location of Bala's first station on the through route, which ran along the southern shore of Llyn Tegid, meant that the station was some distance from the town and attention turned to taking the railway closer. However, providing a small Merionethshire town with more convenient access to the railway was really only an incidental benefit of efforts to secure a far bigger prize – independent access to the slate industry in the Blaenau Ffestiniog area for the Great Western Railway, from which it could then provide the most direct route to the Midlands of England and beyond to London.

An Act of June 1873 authorised the construction of a Bala & Festiniog Railway. This was a nominally independent concern but in practice heavily backed by the Great Western (Sir Daniel Gooch was the company's chairman) and the other interests behind the three companies which had built the railway from Ruabon. After many challenges of taking the railway through difficult terrain, especially the mountainous section beyond Arenig and Trawsfynydd, the line was opened to Llan Ffestiniog in November 1882. Here it met the Festiniog & Blaenau Railway, a narrow-gauge line opened in May 1868 primarily to convey slate from the quarries in the area to Blaenau Ffestiniog for onward transport to Porthmadog via the Festiniog Railway. Transhipment at Llan Ffestiniog was never going to be a viable option in the long term and so a contract was let for the conversion of the narrow-gauge line to standard gauge. In a process which anticipated the famous gauge conversion of the Great Western's remaining broad-gauge lines nearly a decade later, traffic was maintained during the conversion work leading up to a final five-day changeover in September 1883.

The volume of traffic to the artillery training camp and range, opened at Trawsfynydd in 1903, necessitated the construction of a separate military station with two platforms and a siding to permit the efficient handling of large numbers of men, horses and artillery pieces. The military station was located on the Blaenau Ffestiniog side of the public station.

The decline in the use of slate as a roofing material, along with the increased use of road transport from the 1920s onwards which allowed direct transfers from quarry to building site, meant that traffic on the line never really reached the expectations of the original promoters and, with the exception of the periodic military trains, was characteristic of a rural branch-line rather than a major freight route. However, it was the growing demand for water and electricity in the second half of the twentieth century which overshadowed the closure of most of the line and the construction of a completely new piece of railway.

In the 1880s, Liverpool Corporation had constructed a major reservoir, Lake Vyrnwy, to the south of Bala. As the city's requirements grew, it again turned to the area around Bala and identified the Tryweryn valley north of the town as a suitable site for a new reservoir. Parliamentary powers were obtained in 1956 and construction took place over the following decade, a controversial act which invigorated post-war Welsh political identity and activism. The significance for the railway was that a section of the route would be flooded. As part of their planning for the reservoir, Liverpool Corporation surveyed a suitable deviation but this was ultimately not required as during the 1950s, prior to the later work of the infamous Dr Beeching, British Railways had acknowledged that there were parts of the network which could never be economically viable and consequently identified a number of lines for closure. Passenger services between Bala and Blaenau Ffestiniog ultimately ceased in January 1960, with freight trains continuing for another year.

The selection in the 1950s of Trawsfynydd Lake as the location for one of Britain's early nuclear power stations meant that there would be a need for a railhead as close as possible to the site. The Bala–Blaenau Ffestiniog line passed nearby, but its impending closure meant that alternative arrangements would have to be made. The solution was to build a completely new piece of railway at Blaenau Ffestiniog to link the former London & North Western (suffixed 'North' by BR) and Great Western ('Central' under BR) stations and to reopen the Bala line as far as Trawsfynydd Lake Halt, just across the A470 from the power station. The link was constructed by British Railways during 1963 and opened in 1964. It was initially used by trains delivering heavy equipment to the power station site and subsequently for the conveyance of nuclear fuel waste to the Sellafield reprocessing plant.

The reopening of the Festiniog Railway to Blaenau Ffestiniog and the construction of a joint BR & FR station on the site of the former Great Western Station meant that the 1963 link saw daily passenger services from 1982 onwards. In 1980, upon the closure of Barmouth Bridge to locomotive-hauled trains, a siding was added at Maentwrog Road to serve as an alternative loading point for traffic from Cooke's explosives works at Penrhyndeudraeth, although by the end of the 1980s this traffic had ceased. From the late 1980s, the scenic potential of the line south of Blaenau Ffestiniog was recognised and the dated summer-only Sunday Shuttle service on the Conwy Valley line was extended southwards to a point just north of the power station siding. In 1989, a temporary platform was built over the siding at Maentwrog Road to allow those passengers wishing to visit the power station to disembark for the short road journey to the site. Following the closure of the power station in 1991, regular trainloads of spent fuel ran until 1995 and a number of excursion trains operated over the line until 1998, after which the line was closed south of Blaenau Ffestiniog.

Now, over ten years later, the line remains intact in case it should be needed to facilitate the delivery or removal of material during the continuing decommissioning and redevelopment of the power station site. There have also been a couple of proposals for preservation schemes, but to date neither of these has progressed beyond the production of promotional material and it is difficult to see how this part of north Wales could realistically sustain another heritage railway operation.

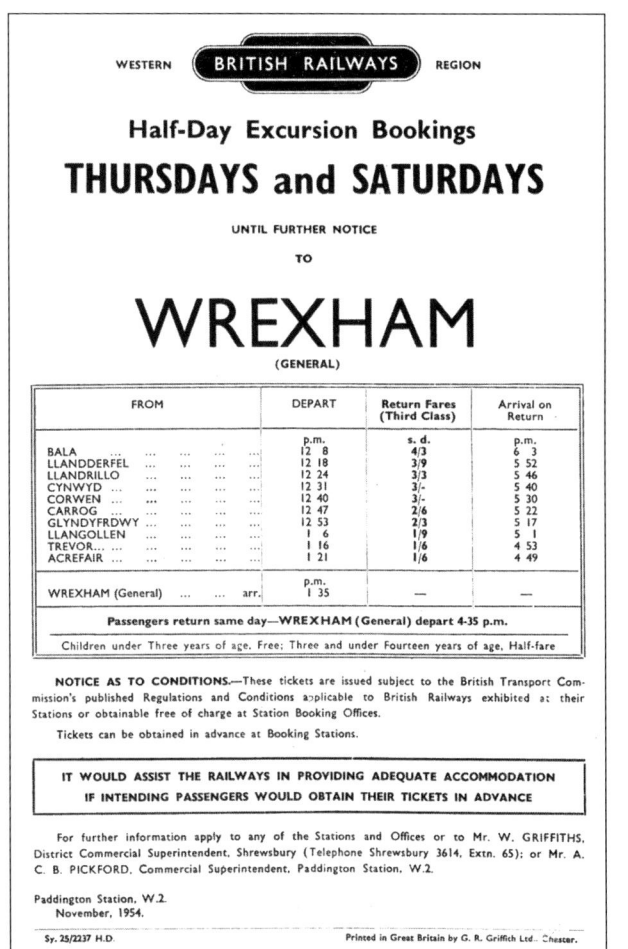

135. Excursion train details, 1954
The timetable and ticket prices for half-day excursions between Bala and Wrexham.

Route description: Bala–Blaenau Ffestiniog

As previously explained, when first opened Bala Junction station was inaccessible except by train, being provided solely for passengers to change to and from branch trains for Bala and Blaenau Ffestiniog. From Bala Junction, the 55-chain section to Bala consisted of two separate single lines; a conventional single line worked by electric train staff and a relief line, essentially a through siding, to the west of it. This arrangement enabled the Chester–Barmouth mail train to serve Bala in the early hours of each morning, without Bala signal box having to be opened. Perhaps the most impressive feature of Bala station was the castellated stone goods warehouse, the elaborate style of which was intended to appease Mr Price of Rhiwlas, an opponent of the railway.

Upon leaving Bala, the line climbed at 1 in 60 to Frongoch (3 miles 23 chains from Bala Junction) which was a block post but did not have facilities for trains to pass. Contemporaneously with the railway, Frongoch was noted first as the location of one of the very few whisky distilleries in Wales and subsequently, located in the former distillery and surrounding grounds, an internment camp was established there for Irish nationalist prisoners following the 1916 Easter Rising.

Beyond Frongoch the line continued to rise with gradients between 1 in 60 and 1 in 300 to Arenig. On this section were halts at Tyddyn Bridge (5–00) and Capel Celyn (6–51) added by the Great Western Railway in 1930 in an attempt to boost patronage. Arenig (8–33) was a passing place and the location of the Arenig Granite Company's quarry, a significant source of freight traffic.

From Arenig, the line climbed further to Cwm Prysor (11–12), a bleak location 1,200 feet above sea level. A passing loop was provided here primarily to improve line capacity for troop trains to Trawsfynydd, with special instructions forbidding ordinary passenger trains from using the loop. Special instructions also governed the preparations to be taken prior to and during periods of heavy snow on this exposed section of line. Beyond Cwm Prysor, the line crossed a substantial viaduct and then ran on a narrow ledge on the hillside before passing halts at Bryncelynog (14–42) and Llafar (15–60) on the descent to Trawsfynydd (17–08), another passing place with goods facilities, a locomotive shed and the separate military station described previously.

From Trawsfynydd, the line descended at 1 in 60 through Trawsfynydd Lake Halt (18–78) to Maentwrog Road (19–75) which, like Frongoch, had goods facilities but was not a passing place. The line then climbed at 1 in 50 to Festiniog (22–03), another passing place with goods facilities. From here onwards to Blaenau Ffestiniog the formation was originally that of the narrow gauge Festiniog & Blaenau Railway and had a number of tight curves. From Festiniog the line rose past Teigl Halt (23–04) to Manod (24–17), another single platform station with sidings. From a point shortly after Manod, the line descended at 1 in 56 to Blaenau Ffestiniog (25–35), terminus of the line and, up to the 1930s, a major traffic interchange with the Festiniog Railway and the various quarries of the district.

Between Manod and Blaenau Ffestiniog there were intermediate sidings at Pengwern, Glan-y-Gors and Tan-y-Manod for stone and slate traffic. Of these Tan-y-Manod (24–65) was the most significant and was also the location of the Great Western's locomotive shed and turntable, meaning that there were additional light-engine movements over the half-mile section between here and Blaenau Ffestiniog.

At the time of going to press, proposals were being considered to introduce a velorail operation on the line. The concept of allowing visitors to enjoy the scenic attractions of closed lines while pedalling their own private rail vehicle is well established in France but would be a novel addition to the tourist attractions of Snowdonia.

136. Timetables, 1950

In 1950, three local services from Ruabon or beyond, terminating at Llangollen, still ran, as did the term-time only service taking scholars from Drws-y-nant and intermediate stations to and from the secondary school in Dolgellau. Over the full route from Ruabon to Barmouth the core (M–F) service consisted of five trains in each direction as well as three services in each direction linking Bala with Ruabon. On Saturdays (SO) up to three additional through services ran in each direction, most without any advertised stops between Ruabon and Dolgellau.

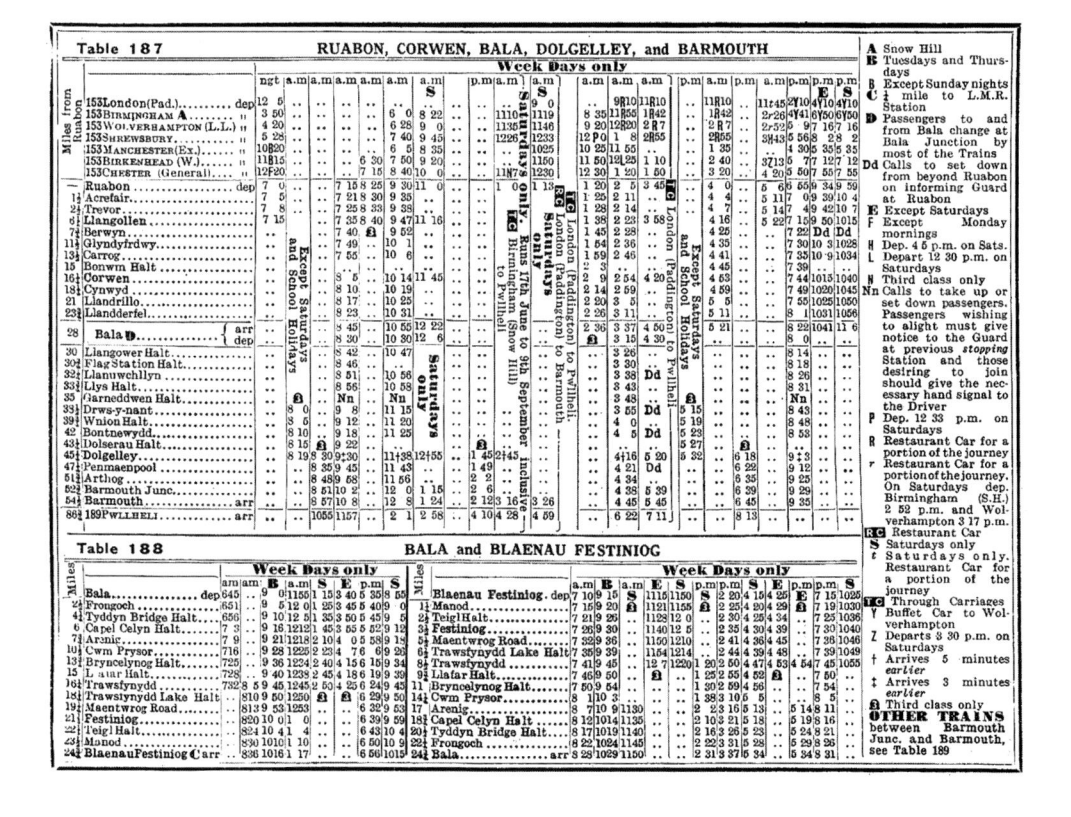

137. BALA, *c.*1950s
The simple, but limited, facilities for locomotives and men at Bala are illustrated in this view looking towards Bala Junction. The small single road shed results in locos standing on the siding on the left. There is an ample supply of loco coal in the wagons on the other siding from which the men had to coal their locos by hand. Bala was a sub-shed to Wrexham Croes Newydd, coded 84J in the original BR classification and changed to 89B in January 1961 and 6C in September 1963. [W. A. Camwell]

138. BALA, *c.*1950s
A closer view of the rudimentary shelter, which provided some protection for the men engaged coaling their locomotives. It is to be hoped that its design took account of the prevailing winds! Note the milepost indicating the half-mile distance to Bala Junction.
[Late B. J. Dobbs]

Rails Through Bala 97

139. BALA, 1958
Former GWR pannier tank N⁰· 4683 prepares to take water from the tank located on top of the single road shed. The ladder on the right gave access to the tank and the hose was just inside the shed. A lamp room and tool shed can be seen on the left, while the limited clearance sign is a reminder to loco crews to keep inside the cab while entering the shed. 16 April 1958. [H.B. Priestley/Pacer Archives]

140. BALA, 1959
Pannier tank N⁰· 5774 stands alongside the goods shed with a single coach waiting its next turn of duty. This could be a service to Blaenau Ffestiniog or a shuttle to Bala Junction, to connect with Ruabon–Barmouth services. 7 August 1959.   [N.E. Preedy]

141. BALA, *c*.1950s
Stationmaster D. G. Edwards and a group of footplatemen and station staff, together with some Wirral-based enthusiasts who have just completed an authorised brake-van ride, pose alongside Pannier tank N⁰· 5774.
[M.E.M. Lloyd/D. Southern Collection]

142. BALA, *c*.1950s
Pannier tank N⁰· 4617 about to leave for Bala Junction with a freight train. The signalman is standing on the boarded crossing awaiting surrender of the single line token from the arrivig train almost hidden by the signal post. The freight train is signalled via the relief line or through siding, a separate bi-directional line running parallel to the passenger line which could be used without the need for a token. Procedures for the use of the relief line were set out in the Sectional Appendix. [M.E.M. Lloyd/D. Southern Collection]

143. BALA, 1964
When this photograph was taken it was the well-made station sign which was the centre of attention. However today's reader will probably regard the classic Thames 'Anglia-style' van as the star attraction. [H.J. Leadbetter]

144. BALA, c.1900s
This classic Edwardian view looking up the Blaenau Ffestiniog branch, has many more people in than later views. The single wheel porters' trolley in the foreground adds interest to the scene. [Heyday Publishing]

145. BALA, c.1920s

Another early view of the station with GWR 517 class 0-4-2T, N° 539, at the head of a train comprised of four- and six-wheeled coaches. On the up platform, behind the train, is the original signal box, closed in 1923. Visible on the approach road is a horse-drawn dray loaded with milk churns and a horse-drawn omnibus, which provided a service to Bala High Street. [Lens of Sutton]

146. BALA, *c.*1950s
Pannier tank N[o.] 5789 stands at the down platform with a passenger train. Note the well-filled bunker. [Stephenson Locomotive Society]

147. BALA, 1958
A view of the distinctive goods shed that was 38-feet long and served by a one-ton crane inside. Of particular note is the castellated stonework provided to please local landowner, Mr Price of Rhiwlas, who had initially opposed the building of the railway. 25 January 1958. [M.E.M. Lloyd/H.J. Leadbetter Collection]

148. BALA, *c*.1950s
Pannier Nº 5774 is seen entering the up loop with a single-coach train from Blaenau Ffestiniog. The area where the permanent way gang's hut is located is now a housing development. [Kidderminster Railway Museum]

149. BALA, *c*.1964
The photographer's son posing alongside BR standard tank Nº 80104 is well wrapped up against the inclement weather, as is the footplateman keeping a watchful eye on him. The footbridge appears to be out of use, which would entail all trains using the down platform. [M.E.M. Lloyd/D. Southern Collection]

150. BALA, 1959
Pannier tank N[o.] 7428, with the GWR initials still visible on its tank, departs for Bala Junction with a single-coach train. 30 March 1959. [Gavin Morrison]

151. BALA, 1959
A busy scene at Bala, with pannier tank N[o.] 7428 going on shed while N[o.] 8727 at the down platform is going to pick up the next working to Bala Junction. 29 March 1959. [Gavin Morrison]

152. BALA, 1961
The hand-operated turntable at Bala was 45-feet in diameter and was used by pannier tanks and 14xx class locomotives. 29 January 1961. [E.N. Bellass]

153. BALA, *c*.1950s
The single-road loco shed at Bala with its overhead water tank is shown to good effect in this close up view. Note the 'Limited Clearance' notice on the left-hand pillar.
[M.E.M. Lloyd/
D. Southern Collection]

Rails Through Bala 105

154. BALA, 1961
Dramatic scenes at Bala as enthusiasts witness the arrival of the final passenger train from Blaenau Ffestiniog. So many people wanted to travel that the much-strengthened train had to be double headed by two pannier tanks with N⁰· 9669 leading. 22 January 1961. [E. Frangleton]

155. FRONGOCH, *c.*1950s
0-6-0 pannier tank, N⁰· 9793, with one coach stands at Frongoch. Of note is the decorative support bracket to the station canopy and the fact that the driver and fireman have time to chat in the sunshine after collecting the staff for proceeding to Bala. [C.L. Caddy]

156. FRONGOCH, 1953
Another Bala-bound train waits as the fireman keeps a watchful eye on the platform through the open door of the toplight-pattern coach. 15 August 1953.   [H.C. Casserley]

157. FRONGOCH, c.1910
An interesting scene in the goods yard as a group of civilians and railway staff gather alongside loaded wagons, the first of which is loaded with whiskey, produced at the local distillery, and also includes a military presence. Note that the adjacent track is keyed on the inside.   [Gwynedd Archives]

158. FRONGOCH, *c.*1950s
A close up view of the signal box and nameboard. [Dave Lawrence-Hugh Davies/'Photos from the Fifties']

159. FRONGOCH, undated
Another casual scene depicted in this commercial postcard. The signal is off, but the guard has time to chat with a man standing with a little girl on the platform. [Author's Collection]

160. FRONGOCH, 1960s
A view taken after closure and track lifting, looking down towards the former goods shed. The station building here was sold off for private occupancy and the absence of vandalism to the signal box shows they are perhaps already in residence. Their restoration works subsequently included the provision of railway-style crossing gates. [R. Icke]

161. TYDDYN BRIDGE HALT, 1957
In the 1930s in an attempt to attract traffic from the burgeoning bus services in rural areas, the GWR built simple halts on many of their country routes. The platforms were usually constructed using second-hand sleepers supporting a simple ash platform, although this one is all timber. The waiting shelters appeared to vary from a simple wooden structure at the more rural locations, the corrugated-iron shelter with curved roof seen here, to the iconic GWR pagoda-style in corrugated iron at busier locations. A nameboard and lamp completed the ensemble, the lamp being lit by the guard of the last train before darkness and put out by the guard of the last train of the day. Clearly such practices preceded the age of the vandal! [Liverpool City Council]

162. CAPEL CELYN HALT, 1961
A view after closure to passengers. 21 January 1961. This halt was primarily for those taking walks under Arenig Mountain but also served the village of Capel Celyn by footpath. A two-coach train also ran to transport school children attending the secondary school in Bala.   [D.K. Jones]

163. ARENIG, *c*.1950
A view of the down platform at Arenig, showing the main station building, signal box, water tower and, beyond that, the gantry and conveyor for carrying quarried stone to the storage hoppers on the up side of the line.
[H.C. Casserley]

110   *Rails Through Bala*

14. ARENIG, 1960
Former Great Western Railway 0-6-0 pannier tank, Nº. 4617, takes on water on 23 April 1960. By this time the line had closed to passenger services.
[M.E.M. Lloyd / D. Southern Collection]

Rails Through Bala 111

165. ARENIG, *c*.1950
A close-up view of the signal box, showing the slate-covered gable end; necessary to cope with the weather conditions sometimes encountered on this line. [Gavin Morrison]

166. ARENIG, *c*.1965
A view after closure when the station buildings were used as a quarry office and quarry plant had been installed on the former track bed. [H.C. Casserley]

167. ARENIG, 1959
The quarry building beyond the railway fence dwarfs the conical water tower on the up platform.
[M.E.M. Lloyd/D. Southern Collection]

168. ARENIG, 1961
Pannier tanks N[os.] 4645 & 9669, in charge of the 'SLS Special – Last Passenger Train' from Bala to Blaenau Ffestiniog make a water stop at Arenig on 22 January.
[W.J. House/C.L. Caddy Collection]

Rails Through Bala 113

169. ARENIG, 1961
A view towards Blaenau Ffestiniog, showing the general track layout after closure to passengers, when the up platform road had been taken out. A feature of the workings at Arenig was that the blasting operations in the quarry could only take place at certain times and written notice had to be given to the person in charge of the station one hour before commencement. A red flag was displayed at the quarry and a green flag at the station when permission was given. On completion the line had to be inspected by the local ganger.
[M.E.M. Lloyd/D. Southern Collection]

170. ARENIG, c.1950s
A closer view of the down starting signal at Arenig surmounting the short-arm shunt signal. Beyond can be noted the substantial stone piers supporting the conveyor and a line of loaded ballast wagons in the yard.
[M.E.M. Lloyd/D. Southern Collection]

171. ARENIG, c.1950s

0-6-0 pannier tank No. 7414 takes water, whilst heading a typical single-coach branch train, under the watchful eye of a member of the station staff. Note the token catcher at the end of the up platform. [Mike Esau]

Rails Through Bala 115

172. ARENIG, *c*.1950s
In this later view the signalman exchanges the Frongoch–Arenig staff for the Arenig–Trawsfynydd staff to a passenger train also conveying a cement wagon. [E.N. Bellass]

173. ARENIG, *c*.1950s
This tranquil view taken beyond the quarry buildings illustrates the isolation of the station as the Afon Tryweryn meanders past the up platform with its simple wooden waiting shelter. [H.B. Priestley/Pacer Archives]

174. ARENIG, *c.*1900
An early posed photograph taken before the opening of the quarry showing clearly both the up and down platforms and a gathering of station staff. [Authors' Collection]

175. ARENIG – CWM PRYSOR, 2005
The trackbed of the line between these locations has now been converted to a public footpath for the benefit of walkers. Where the former bridges have been taken out, footbridges have been provided. [D. Southern]

Rails Through Bala 117

176. CWM PRYSOR HALT, 1950s
A halt was created at Cwm Prysor where a road crossing, with keeper's cottage, already existed. Unlike most other halts, a passing loop and signalling was provided, giving it almost the status of a station. This measure enabled the long-block section between Arenig and Trawsfynydd to be split, primarily for freight and military trains. Service trains were not allowed to cross here. The platform here was also supported by brickwork. The halt served local farms and also Llyn Tryweryn, which was popular with fishermen. The loop was taken out, followed by closure of the signal box on 16 June 1951. [A.Vaughan Collection]

177. CWM PRYSOR, 1961
On 27 January 1961, the crossing keeper is seen opening the gates at this remote location, which is fortunately free from snow on this occasion. [M.E.M. Lloyd/D. Southern Collection]

178. CWM PRYSOR, undated
At 1,200 feet above sea level Cwm Prysor was the highest point on the line. As a result, the line was sometimes blocked by snow in the winter. In this view a locomotive can just be spotted in the distance, presumably on a mission to free the stranded train. Note that the signals are pulled off in both directions indicating that the signal box is switched out. [C.L. Caddy]

179. CWM PRYSOR HALT, 1957
The remoteness of the location is amplified in this view as pannier tank Nº 4645 arrives at the deserted platform with the 12.45 p.m. ex Trawsfyndd (Saturdays only) single-coach train for Bala. 25 August 1957.
[M.E.M. Lloyd/D. Southern Collection]

180. CWM PRYSOR, 1960
0-6-0 pannier tank, Nº 3749, stands at the platform with a freight train for Bala. The year is 1960, passenger services have ceased and the waiting shelter and nameboard have been removed. Note the lever frame for securing the gates. [S.C.L. Phillips]

181. CWM PRYSOR, 1960
A view from the road from where the wicket gate for pedestrians is also visible, as well as an Austin car and a Humber car. [Late B. J. Dobbs]

182. CWM PRYSOR, undated
An interesting period view believed to have been taken before 1915. The lady holding the flag is Harriet James, who from the 1890s to 1926 ran two stations on the line with her husband Robert. They occupied the station house at Trawsfynydd and Mrs James regularly cycled five miles uphill to operate the crossing gates at Cwm Prysor after 1902. On her retirement at the age of 65 the managers presented her with an armchair.
[Courtesy of Gwilym James]

183. CWM PRYSOR VIADUCT, 1959
A view from the carriage window showing the curving nature if the line at this location. Note also the rebuilt top walls and railings fitted earlier in the 1950s. 3 March 1959. [Gavin Morrison]

184. CWM PRYSOR VIADUCT, 1960
0-6-0 pannier tank, N$^o.$ 461,7 crosses the viaduct with a short freight train 6 August 1960. Note the check rail added because of the curve. [M.E.M. Lloyd/D. Southern Collection]

185. BETWEEN CWM PRYSOR AND BRYNCELYNOG, 1959
Another view from the carriage window as 0-6-0 pannier tank N⁰· 8727 heads a one-coach train for Bala along the high shelf at this location. Note the rock wall on the left and the steep drop of some 300 feet to the valley floor on the right. [R.M. Casserley]

186. BETWEEN CWM PRYSOR AND TRAWSFYNDD, 1950s
0-4-2 tank, N⁰· 5810, with the ubiquitous one-coach train between Trawsfyndd and Cwm Prysor. A gangers' motorised trolley is berthed at right angles to the main track. These were provided at strategic locations and there were special token release arrangements to enable the trolleys to be used between trains for safety and maintenance requirements. [J.S. Gilks]

187. BRYNCELYNOG HALT, 1959
As the railway descended from the steep ledge cut into the side of the mountain beyond Cwm Prysor, Bryncelynog Halt was reached. Serving a few scattered and isolated farms in the valley, the halt was opened by the GWR on 13 March 1939. This view on 4 September 1959. [M. Hale, courtesy of G.W. Society]

188. LLAFAR HALT, 1959
A view of Llafar Halt, looking towards Blaenau Ffestiniog, as seen from the end coach of a Bala-bound train on 20 March 1959. [H.C. Casserley]

189. TRAWSFYNYDD, c.1885

This early view shows Armstrong 0-4-2, Nº 1474, with a rake of vintage stock while station staff and family members pose on the platform. In the foreground are the permanent-way gang with their hand trolley
[John Thomas/National Library of Wales]

Rails Through Bala 125

190. TRAWSFYNYDD, 1954
Pannier tank N⁰· 7442 approaches Trawsfynydd with a two-coach train comprising former GWR coaches. The coaches may still be in GWR livery, which survived on the branch for some time after nationalisation. July 1954.
[P.B. Whitehouse]

191. TRAWSFYNYDD, *c*.1912
A view showing the new brick signal box replacing the wooden structure shown in photograph 183. The box was built in connection with the opening of the military station in 1911. It is not known why the goods train is 'wrong road' but it could be shunting back into the military station, the connection for this being beyond the bridge.
[Lens of Sutton]

192. TRAWSFYNYDD, 1959

Time for passengers to stretch their legs as the fireman holds the bag to fill the tanks of pannier No. 7428, while the driver stands ready to turn off the water. The tank supplying the water crane is visible behind the coach. 30 March 1959. [Gavin Morrison]

193. TRAWSFYNYDD, *c*.1911
A passenger train of six-wheeled stock departs on the up line, while the loco on the down line is shunting into the yard. Workmen on the down platform take a break from their job of relaying paving stones. [Lens of Sutton]

194. TRAWSFYNYDD, 1959
After filling the tanks the driver and fireman pose for a photograph while two schoolboy spotters look on. 30 March 1959. [Gavin Morrison]

128 Rails Through Bala

195. TRAWSFYNYDD, 1950s
Pannier tank N⁰· 3689 stands at Trawsfynydd with a short freight. Visible under the arch of the bridge are some cement wagons stabled on the head shunt of the former military station. This was common practice once that station had closed. [G. Harrop]

196. TRAWSFYNYDD, *c*.1957
Pannier tank N⁰· 9793 takes water while working a single-coach train to Bala. The signalman watches proceedings from the opposite platform, while behind him is visible the bracket signal controlling access to the military station behind the bridge. [J.W.T. House/C.L. Caddy Collection]

197. TRAWSFYNYDD, 1959
A view of the goods shed with the signal box and cattle dock in the foreground. The lean-to on the side of the goods shed acted as the loco shed and could house one small loco such as a pannier tank. 3 April 1959. [J.A. Peden]

198. (below right) TRAWSFYNYDD, 1961
Pannier tank No. 9752 stands inside the lean-to shed on the last day of passenger service on the line. 22 January 1961. [J.M. Bentley]

199. (below left) TRAWSFYNYDD, 1961
Pannier tank No. 9752 takes water while working a freight train to Blaenau Ffestiniog. [M.E.M. Lloyd/D. Southern Collection]

130 *Rails Through Bala*

200. TRAWSFYNYDD, 1907
An accident to the train being run for the 53rd Battery, Royal Field Artillery (RFA). During shunting manoeuvres the train had been split into two portions. Unfortunately, the hand brake had not been applied to the first portion, so that, when the loco attempted to buffer up to it, the portion was propelled into the second portion with considerable force. 29 August 1907. [Gwynedd Archives]

201. TRAWSFYNYDD, 1907
A further view of the accident, showing the damaged vehicles moved to one side awaiting disposal, while work continues to repair the track. A gun and the remains of a coach are visible in the wreckage. [Authors' collection]

202. TRAWSFYNYDD MILITARY STATION, *c.*1915
Two trains stand at the military platforms; one having conveyed troops, while the second was for the horses. The field guns and ammunition limbers have been assembled on the platform ready to be moved to the camp. [Authors' Collection]

203. TRAWSFYNYDD MILITARY STATION, *c.*1915
Two GWR saddle tanks head a mixed train for the Royal Field Artillery (RFA) camp, and troops, horses and guns are seen during unloading. [Lens of Sutton]

132 Rails Through Bala

204. TRAWSFYNDD MILITARY STATION, *c*.1915
Yet another busy scene as men, horses and stores are unloaded and assembled prior to transfer to the camp. [Authors' Collection]

205. TRAWSFYNYDD MILITARY STATION, *c*.1930s.
A close-up view of a train loaded with field guns, with a GWR 2-6-0 at the head. [Authors' Collection]

206. TRAWSFYNYDD, c.1910
This view shows that, when dealing with livestock, things do not always go to plan. The horse has probably been frightened by the sound of escaping steam from the loco taking water on the adjacent platform, or perhaps it just does not like travelling by train. [Gwynedd Archives]

207. TRAWSFYNYDD ARTILLERY CAMP AND STATION
A general view of the camp with some permanent buildings and the bell tents, while the field guns are assembled in neat rows. [Authors' Collection]

134 Rails Through Bala

208. TRAWSFYNYDD ARTILLERY CAMP AND STATION
Troops being marched away from a recently arrived train under the watchful gaze of some locals.
[Authors' Collection]

209. TRAWSFYNYDD MILITARY STATION, 1957
The military traffic is long gone in this view of the deserted station, which clearly shows the wide platforms and impressive bracket signals. Cement wagons were often stabled here due to a shortage of space in the goods yard. 29 June 1957. [M.E.M. Lloyd/D. Southern Collection]

210. TRAWSFYNYDD LAKE HALT, 1953
As an alternative to corrugated iron, a modest timber shelter was sometimes provided at more remote halts. It is not clear whether the two passengers and dog are joining or leaving the train, but the guard is keeping a watching brief. [H.C. Casserley]

211. MAENTWROG ROAD, 1957
0-6-0 pannier tank Nº 7442 arrives with a typical one-coach branch train bound for Blaenau Ffestiniog. The nameboard suggests the station is a suitable interchange location for Tan-y-Bwlch station on the Festiniog Railway, some three miles distant. [H.B. Priestley/Pacer Archives]

136 *Rails Through Bala*

212. MAENTWROG ROAD, 1959
A view of the station building taken from the road overbridge. The detached building is the former signal box, which closed *c*.1903. [M.E.M. Lloyd/D. Southern Collection]

213. MAENTWROG ROAD, *c*.1950s
0-6-0 Pannier tank N⁰· 7431 calls with its one-coach train. Two passengers await on the platform. There would appear to have been room for a passing loop should traffic have ever justified it. [G.W. Society Collection]

214. MAENTWROG ROAD, 1959
The goods yard consisted of a single lead from the Bala direction with a headshunt. This served the goods shed and cattle dock whilst coal was dropped at the far end of the siding. [M.E.M. Lloyd/D. Southern Collection]

215. NEAR FFESTINIOG, 1948
0-6-0 pannier tank N⁰· 7431, with a mixed train, displays its number on the buffer beam in GWR style. Several locomotives and coaching stock on the branch continued to carry their old liveries for some time after nationalisation. 20 September 1948. [C.F. Oldham]

138 *Rails Through Bala*

216 & 217. BETWEEN MAENTWROG ROAD AND FESTINIOG, 1960s
An unusual feature could be found in this primitive aqueduct, which carried a stream across the railway.
[John Thomas]

218. FESTINIOG, 1956
A two-coach train hauled by ex GWR 0-4-2T, N⁰· 5810, arrives at Festiniog. Note the substantial station building and the tidy garden in the days when staff had time to tend such things. Note also the poster advertising Newquay, hardly a convenient railway journey for any potential holidaymaker! 1 August 1956. [H.B. Priestley/Pacer Archives]

219. FESTINIOG, 1958
0-6-0 pannier tank N⁰· 7414 heading the 9.35 a.m. goods from Bala, waits to pass class mate 7442 with the reverse working to Bala. 12 May 1958. [J.S. Gilks]

220. FFESTINIOG, 1963
An overall view taken after the end of passenger services with most of the infrastructure still intact
[H.J. Leadbetter]

221. FFESTINIOG, 1963
The signal cabin was provided by the contractors to the original Festiniog & Blaenau Railway and is clad with slate on the gable wall as further weather proofing in this exposed location. [M.E.M. Lloyd/D. Southern Collection]

222. FESTINIOG, *c*.1918
A pre-grouping view of the Blaenau Ffestiniog end of the goods yard with slates waiting to be loaded into wagons belonging to the Great Western, Midland, and the London, Brighton & South Coast railways. Also of note is the early solid-tyred road lorry. [Elfed P. Williams]

142 *Rails Through Bala*

223. FFESTINIOG, c.1920
This early view illustrates the station in its heyday with a cattle dock and ancillary buildings in the yard and a footbridge between the platforms. Unlike many stations it is in close proximity to the village it served. [Authors' collection]

Rails Through Bala 143

223. FFESTINIOG, 1962
A view, looking towards Trawsfyndd, of the abandoned station and the signal box taken shortly after closure. [R. Icke]

225. FESTINIOG, 1950s
The main station building on the down platform. The pagoda hut in the yard, used here as a store, was ultimately recovered to use for its normal purpose of waiting shelter on the preserved Llangollen Railway, initially at Deeside and later at Glyndyfrdwy. [Late W.G. Rear/Authors' Collection]

226. TEIGL HALT, 1952
Former GWR pannier tank N°· 7440 approaches Teigl Halt with the 12.55 p.m. train from Bala to Blaenau Festiniog Central on 13 November 1952. Due to the tight curve on which this halt was built, passengers were requested to travel in the guard's coach at all times for the convenience of setting down. [H. Ballantyne]

227. TEIGL HALT, 1957
Some youthful passengers on the train seem to be very interested in what happens at this location. Access to this remote halt was by a public footpath and the waiting shelter here is of the GWR pagoda style. Note that it has now lost its GWR livery for BR bitumastic black!
[M.E.M. Lloyd/D. Southern Collection]

228. MANOD, *c*.1950s
Certainly not a winter scene as two lightly-clad passengers await their train at Manod, sometimes described as a 'suburb' of Blaenau Ffestiniog, which was only 1½ miles away. [Real Photographs]

229. MANOD, 1953
More typical of the climate here is this scene on a wet 15 August 1953 with the guard looking out as the train departs and the porter heading back to the comfort of the station building. [R.M. Casserley]

230. MANOD, *c*.1950s
A view from the Blaenau Ffestiniog end of the station on a sunny day, showing the wooden cabin over the ground frame controlling access to the two sidings forming the modest goods yard. [T. Oulton]

231. PENGWERN BRANCH, undated
This branch served a granite quarry approximately half a mile from the main line. A train of loaded wagons, hauled by an open-cab pannier tank, is about to cross the main road between Manod and Blaenau Festiniog. A rake of empty wagons of mixed ownership awaits loading in the siding in the foreground. [Authors' Collection]

232. TAN-Y-MANOD, 1957
Another of the ubiquitous pannier tanks rounds the curve at Tan-y-Manod with a mixed freight from Blaenau Ffestiniog to Bala. [M.E.M. Lloyd/D. Southern Collection]

233. TAN-Y-MANOD, 1957
Another view of the curve at Tan-y-Manod showing part of the former engine shed retained to support the water tank servicing the water crane, with a buffer stop installed just beyond the inspection pit. The right-hand track leads to a 45-foot turntable and passes the former loading wharf for the Craig Ddu quarry.
[M.E.M. Lloyd/D. Southern Collection]

234. TAN-Y-MANOD, 1961
0-6-0 pannier tank N° 9752 is seen on the turntable on the last day of freight working between Bala and Blaenau Ffestiniog and return. [M.E.M. Lloyd/D. Southern Collection]

235. BLAENAU FFESTINIOG GAS WORKS, 1961
Blaenau Ffestiniog Gas Works was serviced by coal chutes adjacent to the main line. An engine, with a loaded wagon and brake van, would travel from Blaenau Ffestiniog to Tan-y-Manod, where the engine would be turned, before propelling back to the gas works under the guidance of the guard/shunter for unloading and return to Blaenau Ffestiniog. [M.E.M. Lloyd/D. Southern Collection]

Rails Through Bala 149

236. TAN-Y-MANOD, 1993
The original narrow-gauge line here followed a route round the edge of the valley, which was subsequently shortened by building a timber-trestle viaduct. This had to be replaced by this substantial stone-built structure when the line was converted to standard gauge. Photographed on 21 January 1993. [D. Southern]

237. BOWYDD CROSSING, 1961
Two boys swing on the gate as the crossing keeper closes it after the passage of a train at Bowydd level crossing on the approach to Blaenau Ffestiniog. A porter/signalman from Blaenau Ffestiniog normally worked the gates.
[J. Roberts Collection]

150 *Rails Through Bala*

238. BLAENAU FFESTINIOG, 1961
For sighting purposes the three-arm bracket signal on the approach to Blaenau Ffestiniog was located high on the cutting side. The line passed under the stone arch bridge to the right and the railway land is bounded by a substantial stone wall. [A. Vaughan]

239. BLAENAU FESTINIOG, 1950s
A more general view showing the approach to the bridge. The route follows the alignment of the former narrow-gauge railway between Blaenau Festiniog and Festiniog, hence the curve provided with a check rail.
[Late G.H. Platt]

240. BLAENAU FFESTINIOG, 1957

An overall view of the terminus, with the entry into the goods yard on the left constrained into sharp curves by the limits of the site. There is a gentler curve into the single-platform passenger station and loading dock on the right. The signalbox in the centre of the layout was provided by the GWR in 1925 and replaced a joint GWR/Festiniog Railway box at the far end of the station platform. 29 May 1957.
[M.E.M. Lloyd/D. Southern Collection]

241. BLAENAU FFESTINIOG, 1959

Having run round its train, No. 7428 is ready to depart for Bala. Note the footbridge towards the rear of the platform giving access to the town over the track of the narrow-gauge Festiniog Railway. This section of the Festiniog line was still in use for quarry traffic. 29 March 1959.
[G. Morrison]

242. BLAENAU FFESTINIOG, 1952
0-6-0 pannier tank, Nº 5742, departs with the 11.50 a.m. to Bala. Unusually, the train consists of four coaches, the first two are being worked back to Trawsfynydd ready to form the quarrymen's train the following morning. The last two are the service train. 13 September 1952.
[Industrial Railway Society]

154 *Rails Through Bala*

243. BLAENAU FFESTINIOG, 1959

0-6-0 pannier tank, Nº 7428, still carrying the title GWR on its side, but now fitted with BR-pattern smokebox door numberplate, runs round its single-coach train at Blaenau Ffestiniog Central, the latter word being added by BR to differentiate this station from the former LNWR/LMS terminal in the town. Note the fire buckets on the wall of the gentlemen's toilet. 29 March 1959. [G. Morrison]

Rails Through Bala 155

244. BLAENAU FESTINIOG, 1932
A period view of a train for Bala hauled by open-cab pannier tank N⁰· 1136 with a fine set of clerestory coaches, the first of which appears to be in the maroon livery used by the GWR for a few years.
[R.S. Carpenter Collection]

245. BLAENAU FFESTINIOG, 1949
An unidentified pannier is seen in the loop about to pass a set of quarrymen's coaches which will have formed an early-morning train from Trawsfynydd. The goods shed can be seen with entrances for both narrow- and standard-gauge wagons. In the foreground are empty slate wagons waiting to return to the quarries over the only section of the Festiniog Railway to remain open after the closure of its principal route. 26 July 1949.
[H.B. Priestley/Pacer Archives]

246. BLAENAU FFESTINIOG, *c*.1950s
A view of the substantial station building. This was a single-platform terminal with a run-round loop.
[G.L. Evans]

247. BLAENAU FFESTINIOG, *c*.1950s
A view from the footbridge, showing the station building on the left and the large goods shed in the yard. Note that the track into the narrow-gauge entrance has now been removed. The cement hopper wagons in the siding are probably destined for the construction site of the Trawsfyndd power station that brought much traffic to the line.
[G.L. Evans]

248. BLAENAU FFESTINIOG, 1955
With rows of dressed slates in the foreground, loaded and unloaded, braked and unbraked slate wagons stand on the edge of the main yard. The goods shed can be seen here from the road access side with the loading-bay canopies projecting from the main roof. [Adrian Vaughan Collection]

249. BLAENAU FFESTINIOG, c.1957
A standard gauge 'transporter' wagon used to convey narrow-gauge slate wagons, or trams as they were often referred to, from the wharf at Tan-y-Manod to the main transhipment sidings at Blaenau Ffestiniog. The comb-like projections on the wagon were for attaching chains to secure the trams whilst in transit on the main line.
[M.E.M. Lloyd/
D. Southern Collection)

250. BLAENAU FFESTINIOG, 1959
A view looking along the track of the Festiniog Railway towards the former Great Western Railway station and goods yard, with the narrow-gauge connection curving away to the right. The connection had to cross the standard-gauge headshunt, which by this time was out of use, hence the sleeper laid across the track. 20 March 1959. [H.C. Casserley]

251. BLAENAU FFESTINIOG, 1950
A view taken from the footbridge giving access to the former Great Western station from the town. On the left are slate wagons loaded with what appear to be barrels. The connection to the Festiniog Railway shown previously is in the distance, and the building beyond the standard-gauge headshunt could have been the former signalbox. The Festiniog Railway platform at ground level is centre foreground. 14 September 1950. [R.S. Carpenter]

252. BLAENAU FFESTINIOG, *c.*1957
A two-ton slate tram built by the GWR. Of similar design to those used by the Festiniog railway, it differed mainly by having ten spoke wheels instead of six. Note also the cast number plate and unpainted weight limit plate fitted to the sole bar and the letters GWR cast into the axle grease boxes. It is fitted with a centre-pivoted hand brake.
[H.F. Wheeler]

253. BLAENAU FFESTINIOG, 1959
Prior to 1946 most of the slate quarries in the vicinity of Blaenau Festiniog dispatched their products by the Festiniog Railway direct to Porthmadog Harbour for shipment by sea to their final destinations. With the decline of these facilities this Muir-Hill chain-driven four-wheel locomotive was used to bring slates over the last remaining portion of the Festiniog's 'main line' to the respective yards of the former GWR and LMS (Conway Valley Line) for transhipment. This traffic ceased in November 1962, by which time transfer was being made to motor lorries. [J.A. Peden]

254. BLAENAU FFESTINIOG, 1959
The Muir-Hill is seen here in its working role transporting slate along the Festiniog Railway for transfer to the appropriate main line yard. The loco was constructed by placing a Fordson TVO tractor engine (which was started using petrol) and gearbox on a weighted frame with chain drive to the rail wheels. A rudimentary cab has been added, possibly by the crew. The wagon brake would have been operated by the brakesman riding on the eighth wagon.
[Stephenson Locomotive Society]

255. BLAENAU FFESTINIOG, 1937
No appraisal of the station would be complete without a view (albeit limited) of a passenger train at the Festiniog Railway platform. With two of the diminutive quarrymens' coaches heading the rolling stock, one of the famous double Fairlie locomotives, Taliesin, is in charge. Passenger services ended in 1939 with the commencement of the Second World War. [H.F. Wheeler]

256. BLAENAU FFESTINIOG, 1963
In connection with the construction of a nuclear power station at Trawsfyndd, it was necessary to provide rail facilities to transport the nuclear waste flasks. This was done by constructing a standard-gauge link from the remains of the former GWR line to the Conwy valley branch. In this view a crane is at work during the early stages of the work. [Brian Cowlishaw]

257. BLAENAU FFESTINIOG, 1963
The civil-engineering works for the new link line were extensive, as can be seen here looking back towards the former Blaenau Ffestiniog Central station. [Brian Cowlishaw]

162 Rails Through Bala

258. BLAENAU FFESTINIOG, 1964
Another necessity was the construction of a new road bridge to span both the new link line and the narrow-gauge line, which is seen still intact at this stage.
[Brian Cowlishaw]

259. BLAENAU FFESTINIOG, 1967
The former steam-age branch line enters both the diesel age and the nuclear age as Class 24 N⁰· 5141 passes along the completed link line with a flask train. Locomotives of trains arriving at Blaenau Ffestiniog ran round and propelled it to a siding located to the rear of the former Trawsfynydd Lake Halt, from where the flasks would complete the short journey to the power station by road.
[D. Southern]

Rails Through Bala 163

260. BLAENAU FFESTINIOG, 1997
An added benefit for the residents of Blaenau Ffestiniog was a more central station which also served the preserved Festiniog Railway line to Porthmadog. Here single railcar, No.153313, awaits departure with the 11.48 a.m. to Llandudno in February 1997. [D. Southern]

261. TRAWSFYNYDD, 1995
A flask is seen being unloaded from the rail siding, which had been installed behind the former Trawsfynydd Lake Halt, to road transport for the final journey to the power station. [Paul Shannon]

262. MAENTWROG ROAD, *c*.1967/8
A green liveried Class 24 passes through the station, now in private ownership, with a flask train from Trawsfynydd power station, which can be seen in the background. [N. Gurley]

263. BLAENAU FFESTINIOG, 1988
In addition to the nuclear flask traffic, the new link also generated traffic in explosives which travelled to the siding at Maentwrog Road. A Class 47 passes through the new station with an explosives van protected by barrier wagons. [Paul Shannon]

264. MAENTWROG ROAD, 1989
In the summer months of 1989 and 1990, passengers returned to the former branch line. In a joint initiative between British Rail and Gwynedd County Council, special trains ran initially to Blaenau Ffestiniog but were soon extended to Maentwrog Road. Unable to use the original station, a temporary platform was built in the goods yard. In this view, a five car set can be seen alongside the temporary platform. The North Wales Railway Circle provided a headboard and also a commentary for the benefit of sightseers. [M. Hambly]

265. NEAR FFESTINIOG, 1990
A two-car DMU on one of the Sunday shuttles approaches Ffestiniog. The train is rounding one of the many bends on this section of track since this part of the line follows the route of the former narrow-gauge Festiniog & Blaenau Railway. [D. Southern]

Bibliography

For an understanding of the underlying history of the railways of north Wales and the wider context in which they were conceived, constructed, operated and closed, there is probably nothing better than Peter Baughan's north & mid Wales volume in the *Regional History of the Railways of Great Britain* series (David & Charles, 1980). The corresponding volume in the same publisher's *Forgotten Railways* series, by Rex Christiansen (1976), provides historical facts, contemporary observation and atmosphere supported by a comprehensive gazetteer.

Vic Bradley's *Industrial Locomotives of North Wales* (Industrial Railway Society, 1992), is far more wide-ranging than the title suggests, containing a compact but detailed and comprehensively referenced history of the contractor's operations during the construction of each public railway in the former counties of Clwyd and Gwynedd, in addition to details of all known industrial sites with rail operations of any significance.

Copies of the original drawings for structures at Llangollen, Berwyn and Bala are featured in Frazer Henderson's *The Railway Engineers and Architects of Wales* (National Library of Wales, 1991), written to accompany the National Library's temporary exhibition of the same title.

An internal report on *The Chester Division of the Great Western Railway* (GWR, 1925) provides track plans, details of staffing at each station and commentary on the main traffic flows.

In *The Great Western North of Wolverhampton* (Ian Allan, 1986), Keith Beck devotes a substantial chapter to the Ruabon–Barmouth and Bala–Blaenau Ffestiniog lines in which he gives a particularly detailed account of locomotive allocations and train workings.

Probably most similar in character to the present volume is *Rails to Bala – a Pictorial Survey*, by D.W. Southern, H.J. Leadbetter, M.F. Williams and S.A. Weatherley (Charter, 1987). This was followed by comprehensive pictorial histories of both the Ruabon–Barmouth and Bala–Blaenau Ffestiniog lines from Foxline in their 'Scenes from the Past' series. Bill Rear & Norman Jones wrote *The Llangollen Line – Ruabon to Barmouth* (1990), while Norman Jones assisted Dave Southern with *Bala Junction to Blaenau Ffestiniog* (1995).

As part the Cambrian Railways system, the section between Dolgellau and Morfa Mawddach is covered extensively in the three principal histories of that company; Rex Christiansen & R. W. Miller's *The Cambrian Railways* Volumes 1 & 2 (David & Charles, 1967 & 1971), R. W. Kidner's *The Cambrian Railways* (Oakwood Press, various editions 1954–92) and Volume Two of

C. C. Green's *The Coast Lines of the Cambrian Railways* (Wild Swan, 1996).

The original narrow-gauge Festiniog & Blaenau Railway, which was reconstructed to enable the completion of the Bala–Blaenau Ffestiniog line, is covered in some detail by the leading narrow gauge historian James I. C. Boyd in Volume One of *Narrow Gauge Railways in South Caernarvonshire* (Oakwood, various editions 1972–98).

Since their establishment, both the Llangollen and Bala Lake Railways have published regular magazines for their supporters and several editions of their own guide books for visitors, which in the future may be looked back upon in the same way as today's historians consider the various editions of the publicity material of the Great Western Railway, most notably *North Wales – The British Tyrol – Through the Marches and the Dee Valley to the Sea* (GWR, various editions 1906–24).

The Llangollen Railway has also published two historical volumes covering different sections of the Ruabon–Barmouth line as fundraising activities for locomotive restoration projects, both of which were prepared by Mark Hambly & Dave Southern. *Railways of the Dee Valley* (1989) covered Ruabon to Corwen and *Railways of the Wnion Valley and the Mawddach Estuary* (1991) covered Garneddwen to Morfa Mawddach. The former volume devotes considerable attention to the industrial lines around Acrefair and Trevor and to the Deeside Tramway linking the quarries in the hills above Glyndyfrdwy to the station. In addition, the celebratory *A Return to Glyndyfrdwy* (1992), published to mark the extension of the heritage line to the village of that name, covered probably the shortest-lived piece of railway associated with the line – the temporary tramway laid to facilitate the delivery of the girders for the new bridge built over the Dee there in 1932.

In an age when much excellent material (and some of much more doubtful value) is available on the internet, there are three websites which deserve a particular mention here:

• The history pages of www.llangollen-railway.org.uk, the enthusiast and archive website of the Llangollen Railway.

• Charlie Hulme's www.nwrail.org.uk, an on-line magazine devoted to current news and historical features relating to the railways of north Wales.

• Project Gutenburg, a United States-based project to digitise and make available free of charge out-of-copyright books, offers C. P. Gasquoine's *The Story of the Cambrian – A Biography of a Railway* at www.gutenberg.org/files/20074 which contains an interesting description of early operations on the Cambrian's Dolgellau branch.